A REGULAR GUY

Growing Up With Autism

Landscape Press
833 Topper Lane
Lafayette, CA 94549

Cover art and design, book design: Linda Kalin

www.laurashumaker.com

Printed in U.S.A.

First printing: June 2008

LIBRARY OF CONGRESS CATALOGING-IN-PUBLICATION DATA

Shumaker, Laura
A regular guy: growing up with autism / Laura Shumaker
p. cm.
ISBN-13: 978-0-9801836-0-3
ISBN-10: 0-9801836-0-X

1. Shumaker, Matthew Philbrick. 2. Shumaker, Laura
3. Autism—Patients—Biography 4. Autistic children—Biography
5. Parents of autistic children—Biography
6. Autistic children—Family relationships 7. Mothers and sons
8. Autism   I. Title.

RJ506.A9S58 2008   618.92'85882'00922
QBI07-600341

A REGULAR GUY
Growing Up With Autism

Laura Shumaker

A FAMILY'S STORY OF LOVE AND ACCEPTANCE

LANDSCAPE PRESS
Lafayette, California

CONTENTS

THE ROAD TO THE FUTURE

BEGINNINGS

CHAPTER 1

NERVOUS LAUGHTER

WHEN I WAS EIGHT YEARS OLD, Uncle Russell came to visit. He was my mother's cousin, but everyone called him Uncle Russell. He was twenty years old and had a severe case of cerebral palsy.

Russell was pigeon-toed as I had never seen before, causing his knees to face each other. He walked in a spastic, bouncing stumble. His hands were gnarled and bent at the wrist, fingers curled, in a way that my brother and I found impossible to imitate. His long neck was thick with muscles pulsating from the strain of holding his large, constantly moving head.

Despite his challenges, Russell always had a huge, improbable smile on his face. My brother Scott and I tried in vain not to laugh at him. Even my compassionate mother sometimes had to excuse herself to giggle in the kitchen with us.

"Laura, we'd better not laugh," she said before going back to face poor Russell again. "God may give you one like Russell someday."

Mom wasn't superstitious, and I knew her warning was only meant to sober us enough to get our giggles under control.

Russell wore pointy red Keds and a baggy old cardigan

sweater. His dark hair was greasy, and he smelled bad. I remember thinking that it would sure help if his parents dressed him nicely and cleaned him up a little. Looking back, I realize that his parents did the best they could—the shoes were probably the only ones that fit his feet; cardigans are easier to get on a spastic child than pullovers; and bathing a young man with cerebral palsy is a grueling job for aging parents beaten down by endless caretaking.

Through the years, there were others I couldn't help but laugh at, like the twin brothers at a Christian summer camp when I was fourteen. One was normal and the other weird. The odd boy flapped his hands when he was happy; he'd rock back and forth and sing songs. My friend Ginny and I didn't want to laugh at him, but we found it easier simply to avoid crossing his path so we wouldn't blow it. One time his brother caught my self-conscious giggle and glared at me, deeply hurt. I'll never forget it.

When I was in my twenties and living in San Francisco, I was introduced to a nice-looking guy at a Christmas party. As he stood up to shake my hand, I noticed there was something funny about his legs. He seemed like a great catch—educated, funny, well-dressed except for the bow tie. We sat down again and talked for a while. Eventually, he got my phone number. My excitement turned to dread when he got up to get us a drink. He walked like Uncle Russell. I stifled a nervous, embarrassed laugh and pretended to be laughing at a funny joke I had just heard when he got back with our drinks. Somehow I held it together for the rest of the evening.

He did call me for a date and I accepted. Before he arrived, I told myself that here was a terrific guy with a great attitude who had accomplished much despite his disability, and I should rise above my silliness, be a good person, have a great time. But when I opened the door to greet him and saw him bouncing up the stairs toward my apartment, bouquet of flowers shaking violently, I knew this would be our last date.

I called my mother the next day to share my date story. She didn't laugh.

"I hope you were kind to him," she said quietly. "It must be so hard for him. I'll bet his mother worries."

There was an awkward silence between us, and I felt like a superficial, spoiled brat. What could I say to redeem myself?

"If I had a baby with a problem, it would be hard, but I'd do fine. But I have a feeling my kids are going to be healthy," I said.

"So do I," said Mom. "So do I."

CHAPTER 2

A TRIP TO THE HARDWARE STORE

"MOM! I HAVE SOMETHING VERY IMPORTANT TO TELL YOU," my eighteen-year-old son told me urgently. "We need to go to the hardware store."

I took a deep breath. Another adventure with my autistic son was about to begin.

When we got to the store, Matthew rushed in and disappeared behind the shovels and the toilet seats. I followed, warily. He reappeared with the orange extension cord he'd had in mind.

"Mom, give me the money and let me buy this—like I'm a regular man." His forehead was screwed up with intensity.

I handed him a twenty and told him to meet me outside.

I stood behind Matthew in line, clutching a bottle of Elmer's glue I had grabbed. He wanted me to look like a regular woman, anonymous to him, shopping at Ace Hardware. I watched as Matthew put the extension cord on the counter and handed the saleslady the twenty-dollar bill.

She was Flo, an old-timer with a bouffant hairdo and painted-on eyebrows. I saw the two of them having a little conversation, and I could tell by the confused look on Flo's face that she might need my help. But I held back anxiously to respect Matthew's wishes.

After what seemed like an eternity, Matthew paid for the extension cord and stepped outside to wait for me as I marched up to Flo, placing the glue on the counter.

"See that guy?" she whispered. I glanced out the door and saw Matthew standing there with a self-satisfied look on his face. "He's got mental problems!"

"What did he say?" I asked with a heavy heart.

"He walks up here with his extension cord, and he says, 'Are rhododendrons poisonous to goats?' And I says, 'I don't know.' Then he just starts laughing and walks out with his extension cord!"

"He's my son," I confessed. "I should have explained when I came in. He's autistic."

"Autistic? You mean like the Rain Man?" she asked, looking mortified.

"Well, sort of," I replied. Best not to go into a big explanation right now. "He wanted me to let him buy something at the store like he was a regular guy."

"I feel terrible!" Flo said. "But he must *know* he's different." Realizing that Matthew's hopes, dreams, and lack of self-awareness would be too hard to explain, I shrugged and took my glue.

Flo had no idea how many times I had said to Matthew, "If you want to be treated like a regular guy, you've got to act like a regular guy!" or "Regular guys don't talk about poisonous plants all the time!" Unfortunately, social awkwardness is wired into Matthew's brain, and no amount of instruction or reasoning was going to change that.

I glanced at Matthew as we drove home, and I could tell by the strange smile on his face that he had moved on from his "regular man" frame of mind to the absurd.

"What would happen if Dad ate an oleander?" he asked, grinning crazily, and the lump that had been in my throat on and off since his birth returned.

CHAPTER 3

BEGINNINGS

I DIDN'T NEED TO CHECK my dog-eared copy of *What to Expect When You're Expecting* to know that I was in labor. I had spent the day window-shopping in San Mateo, an upscale community twenty miles south of San Francisco where I lived with my husband Peter. I was proud of my Princess Diana–inspired maternity wardrobe, and on this day I was wearing the red-floral Laura Ashley dress with the ruffled shawl collar that tied in front, sailor-style.

It was 5 p.m., and I was in the bookstore two blocks from home when the first contraction gripped me. Right away, I could tell that my evenings in Lamaze class at our local hospital had been nothing but a social hour.

"Any *day* now!" sang the manager, patting my belly as I hurried from the store.

I made it home in a minute or two, smiling all the way, and called Peter. We were both so excited to become parents.

"They say with the first it takes awhile," Peter said, but he knew from the sound of my voice that I would be an exception. By the time he walked in the door at 6:30, the contractions were three minutes apart. We made it to the hospital at 7:15, and Matthew was born just after midnight, at 12:35. It was May 22, 1986, the happiest day of my life.

I can't remember a time when I didn't know that I wanted to be a mother. I grew up in a loving family with parents who treasured each other. In the beginning, I was the middle child, brother Scott two and a half years older, brother David a year younger. Every evening at five o'clock, the three of us sat on the brick steps of our brown-shingle home in Piedmont, across the bay from San Francisco, waiting for the 42 bus that brought our dad home from his work as a stockbroker in Oakland.

Dad greeted us with a laugh and a hug. Sometimes he'd surprise us with exotic gifts from Chinatown, a few blocks from his office at Dean Witter, where he strolled at lunch: wooden snakes, mystery boxes, fortune cookies. My brothers and I waited in the living room while Mom and Dad had a drink in the kitchen, discussing the events of their day, and we were soothed by the sounds of them laughing and talking. After they had caught up, we were invited in for dinner at the kitchen table. My favorite time of the day followed the evening meal, when I snuggled on the sofa with my mother and we talked or read. Even when I was very small, my mother and I shared private jokes that cemented our bond, and I loved the feeling of our bodies shaking with laughter as we cuddled.

When I was five, my brother David drowned. He was just four years old. I remember standing helplessly on the dock of Clear Lake with my mother and brother Scott while my dad struggled to revive him.

The year that followed his death was quiet and strange. My mother was remote; my father's smile disappeared. Scott and I didn't understand the permanence of David's absence, and we escaped to a world of our own, fantasizing about how David would reappear. One evening, six months after his death, my brother and I found our father crying in our living room, looking at a photograph of beautiful blond David with his clear blue eyes sparkling mischievously.

"Don't worry, Dad," I said, patting his arm. "He'll be back."

"No, Laura. He won't."

And we all wept together. It was the saddest day of my short life, but the day when the healing began for my parents.

Four years later, my father carried my baby sister up the brick steps of our home and put her in an infant seat on the kitchen table, where we all gazed at her sleeping. Carrie was three days old when we adopted her—and once again, we were a family of five. She did not replace David, but she completed our family.

For a nine-year-old girl, there is no more precious gift than a baby, and I relished her completely. After school and on weekends, I spent every moment with her, carrying her around, dressing her, singing to her. When family and friends came to visit the new baby, they had to pry her out of my arms, and they were quick to hand her back while I stood anxiously nearby. "You will be a great mother someday!" Mom told me.

I think I scared away a couple of good prospects when I was in my twenties, with the "Wants to Be a Mother!" stamp on my forehead. Mom told me gently to tone it down a bit, but she admitted that any guy who was afraid of me wasn't the right one anyway.

I spotted Peter at the health club in San Francisco where we were both members. He was dating a friend of mine from college. Peter doesn't remember being introduced to me by his then-girlfriend, but I remember our conversation when he walked away.

"He is so cute! Where did you meet him?" I asked my friend.

Cute was not the proper way to describe Peter. He was handsome, resembling a young Cary Grant with brown hair sweeping across his forehead, a patch of gray in the front. What made him cute was that he didn't know how handsome he was. When I met him he was dressed in jeans and a red crewneck sweater.

"Isn't he *so* East Coast?" my friend gushed. She was hooked. I wondered if he was as well.

When I heard that they had broken up, I found a way to strike up a conversation with him. I noticed an advertisement that he had posted at the gym. His roommate was getting married and he was looking for a new one. I called him and claimed to have a cousin who was moving to the area who might be interested. Our phone conversation turned flirtatious and concluded with a lunch date set for the following day.

Six months into our whirlwind romance, Peter admitted to me that the "Wants to Be a Mother!" sign had scared him at first but ended up being the thing he loved most about me. Peter was one of four kids and had grown up in a devoted family like mine. Nearly all of his family still lived in Connecticut, where he was raised. The old girlfriend was right—he *was* so East Coast.

Peter and I were married only eight months after we met, but nobody was surprised—the love and admiration we shared for one another was obvious.

When we were first married, we lived together in an apartment in the Pacific Heights neighborhood of San Francisco. During the week, we worked, met friends for drinks, and had dinner together, happily making plans for our future. The weekends were spent studying *Gourmet* magazine and having dinner parties with friends.

Shall we use the clay pot tonight or the wok?

Where did you put the eight-inch springform pan?

It's next to the pasta machine in the pantry.

We had season tickets to the ballet; we entered bike and running races. Living in San Francisco was seductive and gave us a false sense of superiority. Looking back, I'm grateful for our self-indulgence. It was a gift to be naive and optimistic. Life would draw us back soon enough.

A baby after two years of marriage was our plan. Matthew beat us by three months.

He was beautiful. We were parents at last.

I was a mother.

CHAPTER 4

THE INTERVIEW

M<small>ATTHEW</small> <small>FUSSED</small> in his infant seat while I struggled to put myself together. In the eight weeks since his birth, I polled my friends who had gone back to work after having had a baby. Wasn't it hard? Didn't you *miss* them? Didn't you feel guilty?

Most of them said it was hard at first, but after a while you got used to it.

"It's so much easier to get errands done. On the way home from work I can pick up the cleaning and groceries," said my friend Jane, "and it's good for my sanity. I need the intellectual stimulation."

I felt plenty stimulated by Matthew, and it wouldn't be any fun going to the cleaners and the grocery store without him. All I needed was the income.

Matthew was a beautiful boy. His round head had just started to sprout straight blond fuzz, filling in the widow's peak that he had from birth. His large brown eyes were framed by golden brows; his lips were full and rosy. I loved looking at him, carrying him around, smelling his silky head and kissing him.

What am I doing?

It was 8 a.m., and time for the good-morning phone call from Mom. I hadn't told her that my job interview was today; if she knew, she would make the one-hour drive so she could watch Matthew for me, and I didn't want to put her through it. And the subject of my going back to work, even part-time, was a sensitive one.

"If it were me, I'd live in a shack before I left my baby to go to work!" she said whenever the subject came up. She hated my response that "most moms these days need to work, especially in the Bay Area."

"But you are not most women," she would say, "and Matthew isn't just any baby."

When I told her about the two-day-a-week job for a pharmaceutical company, even she agreed that if I did have to work, this job would be ideal.

Mom's morning call came while I was fretting over which outfit would best camouflage my huge breasts, especially if they started to leak during the interview. I chose the pink-and-white dress with a stretch waist, and a navy-blue blazer. Matthew, dressed in a brand-new blue-and-white outfit, would be going to the interview with me.

"I just didn't want to get a sitter," I told my mom.

"Laura, how in the world are you going to work if you can't even leave him for this interview?"

"The job doesn't start for a month. I'll be OK by then."

But would I?

Feeling wobbly in my high heels, I pushed Matthew's stroller toward the entrance of a nearby hotel where the interview was to take place, then bolted for the ladies' room where I quickly nursed Matthew to keep him, and my overflowing breasts, quiet for the next 45 minutes. Finally, with my navy blazer still askew, I scanned the lobby for a woman with short frosted hair and a gray suit—Phyllis. She put me at ease right away with her admiration of Matthew. She told me she had interviewed a young mom like me the day before.

"But she only brought pictures! What an honor to meet Matthew in person!"

Does the mom with the pictures want the job? Go ahead and give it to her. I'll be going now.

"Thank you so much," I said. "My babysitter canceled at the last minute."

Phyllis told me that their company had started this flextime program for women like me, who wanted to work in a professional job while raising a family. I would be calling on doctors' offices in my area, telling them about our products and asking that they recommend them to their patients.

"Most women do the job either in two full days, or in three to four mornings a week."

I'm efficient. I can do it in two mornings. Heck, I can probably even take Matthew along.

The interview went well. I boasted about my education and my past experience in sales and got carried away by Phyllis's flattery. In the end, I could see that working for this company made a lot of sense. The job sounded interesting, I could work close to home on a schedule that worked for Matthew and me, and the compensation was great.

"Let's talk about the training," said Phyllis as I handed her my references.

I knew there had to be a catch.

I wasn't at all surprised to see my mother's car parked in front of our apartment when I arrived home. She always had a knack for showing up when I needed her—when the cheerleading list was posted and my name wasn't on it; in the waiting room of my dentist's office after a root canal; when I was single and living in San Francisco and sounded lonely during our morning phone call.

"Awww, poor Laura," she would say. "Let's go for a walk."

My car was still rolling when Mom opened the car door and leaned in to give me a hug. Dad was right behind her, smiling, his eyes fixed on Matthew. My parents were in their mid-fifties when Matthew was born. Dad managed a large brokerage firm in San Francisco, and Mom lived for her new role as grandmother.

I walked into the apartment and saw the laundry I had left in a heap folded in neat stacks on the living room couch. Lunch was waiting for us in the dining room, and the refrigerator was stocked with groceries. I had been gone only two hours.

How had they done it?

I filled my parents in on the interview and told them I was sold on the job until I'd heard about the training.

"One week training—in New York! And it starts in three weeks. There is no way."

"Maybe you can take Matthew with you. Maybe they have

helpers at the hotel."

"I asked, but she said no. She said that if they let one mom do it then all the moms would want to do it, and it would be too complicated."

We sat quietly, all three of us trying to cook up a solution.

"Or Mom and I could fly back with Matthew," said Dad. "We could stay at a different hotel. During breaks you could come see Matthew, and you could spend nights with him. No one has to know. It'll be great fun!"

My mom beamed in agreement.

"You guys, you are so nice," I cried. By now my pink-and-white dress was soaked with perspiration and milk, but I didn't care. "I can't ask you. . . "

But it was no use protesting. Once my parents had an idea, it blossomed quickly.

"Never squelch a generous impulse!" said Dad. It wasn't the first time I'd heard him say that, and it wouldn't be the last.

———

Day one of the training session ended with dinner in the Grand Ballroom, with the group of twenty or so trainees sipping wine and getting to know each other. Most were women like me—in their early thirties, looking polished in their navy-blue suits, high heels, and oversize gold Monet earrings.

"Has anyone seen Laura Shumaker?" asked Phyllis before giving her new trainees a pep talk.

"She just kind of disappeared," said Tina, the one with the baby pictures. "Probably jet lag."

Little did they know that I was at a steak house less than a mile away, cuddling my baby and hearing about all the places he'd been that day with his grandparents.

CHAPTER 5

MATTHEW'S FIRST YEAR

THE WEEK AFTER WE ARRIVED HOME from the training class in New York, Mom and I sat in the dining room table while Matthew napped, narrowing down responses to the ad I had placed in the paper.

"Wanted: Loving care for my three-month-old son, two days a week."

We set up appointments for three respondents that afternoon, and two the next. "I hope you don't mind," said my mom, "but I really want to see these women myself. I'm a good judge of character."

She *was* a good judge of character, but I knew she had another motive. Mom had offered to take care of Matthew while I worked, but it would mean an hour's drive two mornings and afternoons a week, and I worried that the commitment would be too much for her. I also worried that it would put a strain on our relationship.

"If I can't watch him while you're working, I'll be worrying about him, so I might as well," she argued, "and I'll love every minute of it."

"Let's just see who's out there," I said. "You never know."

But one by one Mom eliminated all of the candidates, some for obvious reasons—lack of personality and experience—and others for not-so-obvious reasons.

"Did you see her nails? Do you think a woman with perfect nails cares about anyone more than herself?" or "Behind that big smile is a mean woman."

In the end, I relented and accepted Mom's offer, but just for one day a week. The other day, Matthew would stay with a mom in the neighborhood who had a son Matthew's age and a three-year-old daughter.

"But guess who she'll go to first if they all need her at once," Mom warned. "It won't be Matthew."

As always, Mom softened her barbs with good humor and encouragement. "Just think how fun it will be for me. Just think how much fun it will be for you when Matthew has children of his own!" and "It's good for you to work a little bit. Be sure to keep some of the money you make *just* for yourself."

Peter and I agreed that the best thing about working was coming home to Matthew. His whole body wiggled with joy when he saw us, and his smiles and gurgly laughter were contagious. In the evenings we took walks with him, first in the Snuggli, then in the stroller and the backpack. We smiled proudly when passersby gasped, "What a beautiful baby!" Once home, after we bathed Matthew and put him to bed, we pored through our baby book and compared their estimates of developmental milestones with his.

"They say 'sits up by the end of month four.' He was doing that by the end of month three!" I told Peter.

"It looks like he should be rolling over soon," said Peter, turning the pages, "and then peek-a-boo the next month. Let's try it now. . . . And then in month eight—"

With each month that passed, Matthew's personality sparkled brighter—sunny like the blond hair that stood straight up, impish like his dimply smile, cuddly and warm like his beautiful brown eyes.

We were in love.

CHAPTER 6

LOSS OF INNOCENCE

I REMEMBER the first time I noticed that Matthew was different.

He was about a year old and we were at Gymboree, a program where stir-crazy new mothers could connect while their babies got to tumble and play.

The class was held in the basement of a neighborhood Methodist church that smelled of applesauce cake and burnt coffee. I proudly carried Matthew into the class for the first session. I loved the way he sat on my hip, his arm hooked around mine, and how his legs and arms clung tighter when I leaned down to put him on the red mat with the other babies. Matthew was the cutest baby there.

I chatted with a woman who was dressed in perfect blue jeans and asked the usual questions—"Who is your pediatrician?" "How do you like your stroller?" She stopped mid-sentence and exclaimed, "Look at your little boy! He's fascinated with the wheels on that board!" While the other babies were exploring balls and hula hoops or rolling down padded ramps, Matthew sat on his bottom and studied a 12x12-inch board with wheels on the base.

"Matthew!" I called playfully. He looked up briefly and continued to study the wheels.

"How cute!" the perky mother said. "He'll probably be an engineer someday!"

The other babies gathered with their mothers for the highlight of the session—the unfurling of the parachute—but Matthew stayed with the board, leaning over to get a good look at how the wheels were working.

I picked him up and plopped him on the floor in the circle around the parachute. The moms lifted the multicolored silk parachute up in unison, filling it with air, and huddled underneath, babies in laps, while it floated down on top of us. But Matthew fussed and found his way out of the colorful fort in search of the board and its whirling wheels. All the mothers laughed, and I joined in uneasily.

He's just a baby, I thought. *This is just baby stuff.* But he was the only baby who wouldn't stay with the group.

When I recounted the day to Peter, I framed the board incident in a positive way. I told him about the attractive mother's engineer comment, and that of course Matthew was the cutest baby there.

I remember that the week following that first Gymboree session, I felt mildly anxious about the next. Matthew's penchant for playing with our yellow Mighty Mite vacuum cleaner, wrapping himself with the hose and inspecting the wheels, didn't seem quite so endearing now.

At the next Gymboree session a week later, Matthew went right for the rolling board, and I didn't fight it. I felt isolated as he turned the board over and spun the wheels, one by one, then turned it over again and rolled it around, bending to watch the wheels roll on the shiny wood floor. Meanwhile, the other mothers and babies played and chatted elsewhere in the room. There were a few sideways glances from the group, and my fantasies faded of finding one lifelong friend in the crowd to whom I could say at our kids' high-school graduation: "And just think, we met when they were babies at Gymboree!"

I left a little early and took Matthew for a visit with my mom, who lived across the bay, about thirty minutes away. She had a special bond with her oldest daughter's first child, and I needed a dose of her unconditional love. I told her about our experience with the class, the sideways glances and how I felt pushed out of the loop.

My mother hugged me and said, "They're just jealous because Matthew is so adorable." We laughed about my worries with Matthew's wheel fascination and how it might jeopardize our playgroup eligibility.

"To heck with them!" my mother declared. She reminded me that Matthew was perfect and that I was hormonal.

"You're not the playgroup type anyway!"

We sat outside and talked while Matthew played with the garden hose, the sun on our backs. Mom was so happy I had come by, and the warmth of her love and humor renewed my spirit. I smiled to myself and pushed my doubts about Matthew to the back of my mind, dismissing them as first-time mom jitters. But from that day on, I never looked at him the same way.

CHAPTER 7

"SHOULD I BE WORRIED?"

MATTHEW'S BROTHER ANDY was born May 17, 1988, almost two years to the day after Matthew's birthday of May 22. I had hoped for a girl, and everyone knew it, but my mother pointed out how wonderful it would be for Matthew to have a brother and what a great big brother he would be.

Andy was not the beautiful newborn Matthew had been. He looked like Yoda. When my father first held Andy in the hospital, he inspected him carefully and asked casually, "Was it a tough birth?"

"He'll be all right," my mother assured him, also looking mildly concerned.

"He probably just had a hard time coming around the bend," Dad concluded.

Looking back at videos from that day in the hospital when we introduced Matthew to Andy, we see the people we used to be— full of hope, but unsettled, and trying to hide it. Matthew is a handsome two-year-old with a solid build and golden blond hair, wearing OshKosh overalls and new blue sneakers. He is rolling Andy in his bassinet around the room. We ask him questions about his new brother, and his deep brown eyes flash at us briefly, then return to the rolling bassinet.

"Do you like the new baby, Matthew?"

"Baby, Matthew."

We laugh nervously and then turn the camera off.

We were worried.

Matthew had started talking like other babies at the one-year mark, and then he stopped. In the past year, his gurgly laughter and joyous smiles turned muted and dreamy, and his eyes didn't connect with ours the way they used to.

"Ask the pediatrician what he thinks," suggested Peter.

————————

I scheduled Andy's two-week checkup and Matthew's two-year physical on the same day. Weeks before Andy's birth we'd bought our first home in a suburban community just ten minutes from where my parents lived, thirty miles east of San Francisco. This was only my second meeting with our new pediatrician.

"Don't worry, Mrs. Shumaker," the pediatrician said, gazing distractedly out the window as he listened to Matthew's chest. "Language takes off once they hit two years."

"Well, he's two," I said, "and believe me, his language is not taking off. The funny thing is, he started talking like other babies at around one, but then he stopped."

"Kids often regress when there is a new baby in the family," said the pediatrician. "Don't worry. By the time you come for Andy's next visit, Matthew will be talking so much, you'll want him to shut up!" And with a quick scribble in the baby book, he was off.

Good point about the new baby in the family.

In the months that followed, baby Andy proved to be a wonderful distraction from my constant preoccupation with Matthew's peculiar development. Peter and I were in awe of Andy's emerging personality and his quick and firm grasp of every milestone. In photographs as early as three months, Andy is studying toy trucks and blocks with intensity, but stops to flash a smile and raise an eyebrow when I call his name, his gaze connecting with mine, his eyes shining with joy, my heart overflowing.

But while Andy surged ahead, Matthew lagged, and quirks in his speech and behavior popped up daily. I found myself apologizing to friends when we were invited for playdates, or when visiting the park.

"He's going through a stage where he likes to play with wheels!"

"He's really into lining up toys. Maybe he'll be a graphic artist someday!"

When I asked Matthew a question, if he responded at all, he would repeat what I had said rather than answer.

"Do you want to go on the swing, Matthew?"

"Swing, Matthew."

"What a big boy!"

"Big boy."

"Do you want some juice?"

"Juice."

I asked my friends and random mothers at the park if their children ever did that, repeating everything they said, and they said no.

Waiting and watching, I became impatient as Matthew approached his third year. I had been following the advice of magazines and baby books about how to stimulate language development and was weary from my lack of success.

"Look! You are crawling *under* the table. Watch me jump over the blocks."

"Let's go *up* the stairs. Let's count the stairs one, two, three. Now we'll go *down* the stairs. One, two, three. . . can you count with me?"

Nothing.

Then one hot Friday afternoon a week before his third birthday, Matthew pointed at a stoplight on the way to the grocery store.

"Light," he said. *Is his language taking off?*

"That's right! Light! Red light. Red means stop."

I was getting ahead of myself. *Keep it simple.*

"Red light! Can you say red light?" I continued.

He pointed at the stoplight again and said, "Light."

Cheerfully, "That's right! Red light! Red means stop."

I looked at his precious face in the rearview mirror. He was so passive. Couldn't he show a little enthusiasm?

I proceeded to the next stoplight, and Matthew pointed to it and said, "Light."

"Good boy! Light! Red light. Look! Now the light is green!"

I quickly figured out that I couldn't turn this into a teaching moment. All he could do right now was point and say "Light." All the way to the store. What was going on in his little brain?

Frustrated, I tried to move from lights to trees, houses, cars, anything. Matthew was fixated on the lights. I struggled through the store with Matthew in the cart, pointing at all the lights, while Andy squirmed in the Snuggli. "Light, light, light."

"Isn't that cute!" said the checker. "He just loves the lights! Maybe he'll be an electrician someday!"

On the way home, I took a route with fewer traffic lights—I hadn't realized till today that there were so many in the world—and put Matthew and Andy down for a nap.

While Matthew was asleep, I picked up the phone and dialed an old friend of my parents. He was a child psychologist and a specialist in early childhood development at Stanford University, about an hour south of our home. The last time I had seen him was when Matthew was just two months old, and I had dropped by his office to show Matthew off. I hoped that Dr. Hoffman could quell my anxiety, or offer a suggestion or two.

"Hello, this is Dr. Brian Hoffman. Please leave me a message and I will return your call."

Beep.

"Hi, Brian, this is Laura Shumaker. Baby Andy is doing great and so is Matthew, but I have a quick question. He is not talking as much as most kids his age, and he does this funny thing where he repeats what I say. He's not conversational. Is this normal? Oh, and he gets stuck on things—like lights. Should I be worried?"

There, I've done it.

The next morning Peter and I took the boys for a walk in town so that I could show him the light thing. It wasn't a very long walk, but Matthew continued to find, and point at, every light.

"Light."

We pushed the stroller up the hill toward our house, trying to make sense of Matthew's peculiar obsession. When we arrived home, there was a message from Dr. Hoffman.

"Hello, Laura. I am happy that you are well. What you are describing is called echolalia, and it can be a sign of something very serious. The perseverative behavior also concerns me. You should ask your pediatrician for a referral to a speech therapist. I would be happy to see him as well. Some possible appointment times are. . . "

And that's when it all started.

CHAPTER 8

THE SPEECH LADY

THE NEXT MORNING I decided to do something, and I couldn't stop until I had done everything. I called Dr. Hoffman. When can you see Matthew? Can you fit him in today? He told me that he would prefer to see Matthew after a speech and language evaluation.

I called my pediatrician. Matthew needs a speech and language evaluation. Who do you recommend?

I called the speech therapist. How soon can you see my son? Tomorrow?

That's too soon. I need to work on his vocabulary first.

How about the day after tomorrow? See you then!

Peter and I took turns that day and the next working with Matthew on his vocabulary, hoping that a crash course could make this whole thing go away or at least improve his results in the speech evaluation.

Matthew liked one book in particular, *Richard Scary's Best Word Book Ever!*, and we took full advantage of it, though our tutoring sessions never went the way we hoped. The evening before our visit to the speech therapist, I lurked in the hallway while Peter read to Matthew before bed.

"Let's look at the book, Matthew," said Peter.

"Book, Matthew," he replied.

"See the red car?"

"Red car."

"Can you show me the red car?"

Matthew squirmed away, and Peter's voice grew louder, more desperate.

"Come on, big boy. Just a few more minutes."

He forced Matthew back in his lap and opened the book.

"See the funny worm? He's driving a *car*! Isn't he funny?"

"Light," said Matthew, pointing at the headlights on the car. Peter turned the page.

"Light," said Matthew, pointing to the lamp on the bedside table.

"That right, Matthew," said Peter, closing the book as his frustrated eyes met mine.

"Light."

———

The speech therapist that my pediatrician recommended worked in a clinic at our local hospital. She was young and humorless, and she was the first person who hadn't mentioned how adorable Matthew was.

My only experience with speech therapy had been when I myself was evaluated in the third grade. The "speech lady" had recommended five or so visits to correct a minor lisp. In my circle of friends, I didn't know anyone whose children needed evaluation at this young age, so I half-expected and hoped that this "speech lady" would take a look at Matthew and sign us up for a few corrective sessions.

But when she escorted me into her office, after having worked with Matthew for thirty minutes, it was clear that she wouldn't be signing up to help him.

"He's definitely delayed," she said, shaking her head like an exasperated babysitter waiting to be paid.

"By delayed, do you mean he can catch up?" I asked.

"It depends on what is causing the delay. A good child psychologist or psychiatrist could help you with a diagnosis."

Diagnosis? The speech therapist said that she had a hard time engaging Matthew in any testing activities.

"He avoided eye contact," she said, "and he's clearly echolalic." I remembered that Dr. Hoffman had said that echolalia—repeating, rather than responding to the words and phrases of others—could be the sign of something serious. Now two people had used the word "serious."

And it hit me all at once that this was serious.

". . . so I got out the blocks and he lined them up rather than answer questions about them," she went on, "and he tapped his hands on the table like this," she said, tapping her index finger on the table for about ten seconds.

"He's been doing that. Tapping, and lining up his toys," I said. "He's also fascinated with water going down drains, and sprinklers going on and off," I admitted boldly. Might as well get my money's worth. "But what does that have to do with his language?"

"Whatever is going on here, it's not just his language," she said. "A child psychologist can look at the whole picture. Try this woman," she said, scribbling down a name and number on a pad of paper.

"We know a good child psychologist," I said. "Dr. Hoffman down at Stanford."

"I've heard he's good, but that he doesn't do psychological testing," said the speech therapist. "You can ask him, but I'd try Dr. Davies. She's close by and specializes in diagnostic work. Mention that Matthew has seen me, and that I suspect he's developmentally delayed."

Developmentally delayed.

I drove home, glancing at Matthew's passive face in the rearview mirror while Andy babbled happily in his baby seat beside me. What would having a brother with a serious problem mean to him? I felt angry with Matthew for not being more cooperative with the therapist, and upset with the therapist for not getting the best out of him.

I wonder if she's a mother? If she were a mother, she would have known how to handle him, and she would have been gentler with me. And, damn it, why had my pediatrician sent me blindly to this cold woman after telling me not to worry? It's time to find another pediatrician, one that will take me seriously.

Now, worried and afraid, I sat paralyzed at a stop sign, until a loud horn blared behind me.

Magically, my car found a shady space by the side of the road where I sobbed as long as my boys would let me. Then I drove to my parents' house, where my mom was waiting with a cold washcloth and a hug.

"He's still Matthew," she said. "He's still our sweet Matthew."

CHAPTER 9

FEAR

THAT EVENING, Peter and I sat at the dining room table with a dictionary, a stack of encyclopedias, and an old college textbook on child development. It was time to do a little research.

"Echolalia: ech·o·la·li·a (ĕk´ō-lā´lē-ə) 1. *Psychiatry* The immediate and involuntary repetition of words or phrases just spoken by others, often a symptom of autism."

Autism?

I flipped open my World Book encyclopedia to autism, my heart pounding, and read out loud to Peter.

"A rare, severe developmental disorder that begins before four years of age. The condition appears as a group of symptoms, the most notable of which is the inability to relate socially to other people. True autism occurs in one child in every 700. Boys are more commonly affected than girls. There is no known cure for the condition. The term *autistic* or *autistic like* is sometimes used to describe people with severe emotional problems that resemble autism."

There was more, but I couldn't read it.

"Don't worry, Laura," said Peter, squeezing my hand. "This is just worst-case scenario stuff. There is no way Matthew is *autistic*."

I had first heard the word "autism" when my sixth-grade class went to visit Agnews Developmental Center in Santa Clara, California, where children our age lived because they were emotionally disturbed, mentally ill, or developmentally disabled. I'm sure that the reason for the field trip was to educate us and infuse us with compassion, but instead the trip had a freak-show, haunted-house atmosphere. Students stared and pointed, and teachers seemed unsure, frightened.

During the tour I noticed a tall, handsome boy with a brown bowl haircut rocking in a doorway, mumbling quietly to himself and waving his fingers. He had high cheekbones and clear blue eyes, and he looked a little older than my twelve years, though it was hard to tell because his face was void of expression. It was spooky.

"He's so handsome," I whispered to the tour guide, "but it's like he's looking at me but not seeing me. What's wrong with him?"

"He's autistic," she said. "People with autism are locked in their own world. They have no emotions, and they don't like to be touched."

I overheard one of the mothers who helped supervise the field trip whisper to another, "I hear it's because they have refrigerator mothers—you know, those women who can't love their children."

That would never be me.

Years later, in 1988, the movie *Rain Man* was released, when Matthew was one and a half. In the movie Dustin Hoffman plays Raymond, a severely autistic man, obsessed with routine, who

rocks and screams when his schedule is disrupted. He has difficulty making eye contact and mumbles amazing facts and figures
that have no practical value. The character became the defini-
tion of autism, and everyone was talking about it when it first
came out.

"Isn't it amazing that autistic people are so brilliant with facts
and numbers," people would say, "but so limited otherwise, and
so odd."

Few understood that autism was a wide spectrum disorder,
and that not all autistic people are alike. So when Peter and I met
with the child psychologist who did testing for a consultation,
even before we were seated I blurted out that two professionals
had used the word echolalia.

"Does that mean he's autistic?" I asked.

"Echolalia is only one symptom of autism. A person with
echolalia alone is not necessarily autistic."

"Well, that's a relief!" I said with a sigh.

"We've been a couple of wrecks," Peter said, taking my hand.
"It's so hard not to jump to conclusions!"

Dr. Davies, a stoic English woman in her sixties, gave us no
indication that it was time to celebrate as she looked over the
speech therapist's report. She asked us about pregnancy and birth
(normal, normal) and asked us to list the ages of achievement of
important milestones. I rattled them off like a contestant on a
quiz show.

"I think she's sugarcoating them a little," Peter said, and I
blushed.

"Oh, that's what we mothers do," said Dr. Davies with a slight smile, her eyes connecting briefly with mine. She understood.

Dr. Davies explained that she would use the results from two different tests, the Stanford-Binet Intelligence Scale (SB) and the Bayley Scales of Infant Development (BSID), to get the best reading of Matthew's stage of development. The results would also highlight the areas where Matthew could use remediation.

The testing was done over a two-day period, and each day, Matthew clung to me for a few minutes before allowing Dr. Davies to take his hand and lead him into her office.

"No refrigerator mother here!" I laughed nervously, wiping tears away as I turned over my boy for this clinical evaluation.

"We'll be about 45 minutes," she said with that slight sympathetic smile.

Peter and I met Dr. Davies a final time to go over the test results.

"He is not retarded, and he is not autistic," she proclaimed. "His most obvious problem is that he has a serious language delay, but he also seems to have an overall cognitive delay. But this is secondary to his language delay, and no final diagnosis can be made until he works with a speech and language therapist."

"So do you think that once he gets speech therapy, the cognitive part will come up?" I asked hopefully. "Do you think this is something he can overcome?"

Peter gave me a "don't put words in her mouth" look.

"I don't have a crystal ball. But extensive work with a speech and language therapist, and placement in a remedial preschool, is crucial."

"I heard that you don't see children beyond evaluation, but do you think he would benefit from seeing someone else?" I asked. "We have a family friend, Brian Hoffman, who has offered to see him. Do you know him?"

"Yes, Dr. Hoffman is wonderful," she said, "but there are many in this area who treat children with developmental disabilities as well."

Dr. Davies handed me a sheet with diagnostic information for our insurance and wished us luck.

Did she say disability? What happened to delay?

"What did you make of all that?" Peter asked as we drove home. He sounded discouraged.

"What did I make of it? I think it's good news! We'll pour on the speech therapy—that should get him going—and then if he needs more of a boost, we'll get him to a child psychologist. I'll bet we can turn things around."

"Laura, she never said anything about things getting better. At the very least, it's obvious that he has some major learning disability. She recommended some pretty heavy-duty stuff. This is depressing."

I replied with a sigh.

"Boy, I'd do anything to get Matthew on track," said Peter.

"And we will. Matthew sure is lucky."

Peter turned on some music. I unfolded the piece of paper that Dr. Davies had given me and read it silently. "Diagnosis: DSM-111 R, 1315.31 Developmental expressive language disorder; 315.31 Developmental receptive language disorder; 299.80

Pervasive developmental disorder, not otherwise specified. The latter diagnosis is descriptive of Matthew at the time of the examination. This may well be revised after he has some language therapy."

"What does it say?" asked Peter.

"Just what she said," I sighed. "We'll get him the therapy he needs. I'm tired of talking about it."

I closed my overflowing eyes and turned to the window, keeping my fear to myself.

CHAPTER 10

FRANTIC

IT HAD BEEN A MONTH since our last meeting with Dr. Davies, and I hadn't stopped moving, driving, calling, and worrying. I felt I had a window of opportunity in which to help Matthew catch up. As long as I was doing something, anything, I believed that I was moving Matthew along. My first call the day after our meeting with Dr. Davies had been to Dr. Hoffman.

"I'm out of the office until December 26. . ."

Three weeks! But I need him now!

I left him a message asking if he would meet us on December 27. While waiting for his return, I threw myself into scheduling speech therapy and finding a remedial preschool.

Dr. Davies had steered me away from the speech therapist who had seen Matthew initially, saying that Matthew would do better with a therapist experienced with developmental disabilities. Her name was Christy, and I liked her a lot. She was about my age, smart and energetic. A mother herself, she had a great sense of humor, and she was determined to move Matthew along.

"His expressive and receptive language is severely delayed," she told me. "He should be seen by an audiologist to check his hearing. Some children with speech and language delays have auditory processing problems—their hearing is fine, but their interpretations of the sounds misfire. But in the meantime, let's start with thirty-minute sessions three times a week, and I'll give you exercises to work on at home."

"Could he use more than three?" I pressed. "We can do more. . . "

"Three with the home program is enough," she said. "Let's not overwhelm poor Matthew."

Recently I had reluctantly returned to work as a pharmaceutical representative two or three mornings a week.

"Don't you think I ought to quit and stay home with the boys?" I'd asked Peter. "Especially with all that's going on with Matthew."

"We could if we moved to a part of the country that's less expensive," Peter said.

Before we were married, Peter and I had a romantic notion of traveling in Europe, and then settling down in an area where we could buy a big house and I could stay home with three or four children.

But there had never been a trip to Europe, and now there was no way I was going to move away from my parents—my support system. Peter was doing well in sales for IBM, and I was more confident than he that we wouldn't need my income for long, and I could stay home with my boys. But in the meantime, Matthew and Andy were looked after while I worked by a kind and patient young Peruvian woman—someone my mother liked as much as I did. I had convinced Mom that watching the boys should be a treat, not an obligation, and she agreed.

But Liliana's English needed work.

"That's not so great for the home program, is it, when the kid with the speech problem can speak better English than the babysitter," I said, feeling like a clueless mother.

"If she has connected with your boys, I'd stick with her," Mom said. "Matthew will be in preschool soon, and it won't be an issue."

After each thirty-minute session, I asked Christy how things were going.

"Have you ever met a boy who has overcome such delays?"

"He's progressing," she'd say, and we would go over the victories of the day and review what needed work.

But with progress came frustration.

"He gets stuck on a word, a toy, or a phrase, and he can't get unstuck," said Christy. "If I push him he gets dreamy, and laughs inappropriately. And he reacts to every sound, even remote ones, by looking for its source. I could swear that he hears the guy scooping ice cream at the ice cream parlor two blocks away."

I was frustrated, too. I felt Matthew had the capacity to understand, but he was just fixated on peculiar things, like water going down a drain, lights, cows on the hillside, and sounds— every sound. He also made strange movements—jumping up and down and dipping to touch the ground. When he watched airplanes flying by, he stared intensely, smiled, and flapped his hands very fast. He showed no interest in playing with children his age.

"What should I do when he goes off track like that?" I asked.

"You need to take his hands, get him to look you in the eye, and say, 'That's inappropriate. We are not going to do that right now.'"

Are you kidding? I'd be saying that all day!

With speech therapy well underway, I searched for a remedial preschool. But when I saw the one that the child psychologist Dr. Davies had recommended, I was crushed. The students, all boys, were severely disabled. One little boy was in a wheelchair and wore some sort of breathing apparatus; another appeared to have Down syndrome. What on earth was this? Is this how Dr. Davies had viewed Matthew? This kind of school would only slow him down. He needed to catch up!

I decided on a preschool that young mothers in my neighborhood had raved about. I figured that the best way for Matthew to catch up with children who were developmentally on track was to be with them. He could learn to play and socialize by watching them in action, and maybe he could make a friend or two.

I told his teacher, Gretchen, that Matthew might have a learning disability, but that he was getting a lot of speech therapy and would probably grow out of it. She had years of experience and said she would be happy to work with Matthew; she had even taught children with "special needs," a term I had never heard before. Would his speech therapist like to visit the class and make suggestions?

The first day of preschool, I stayed and observed for about an hour. It was so painful. The morning started with circle time, with all the mothers sitting in a circle with their children in their laps for a song and announcements. I felt like I was back at

Gymboree again, with Matthew squirming out of my lap immediately, this time to play with the water fountain.

"Matthew, why don't you come join us?" urged Gretchen
cheerfully as I scrambled to bring him back.

"Children, this is Matthew Shumaker!" she said. "Let's
welcome Matthew to Merriewood."

The group sang "Getting to Know You," but Matthew didn't
notice, and he got up again to play with the water fountain. I
shrugged cheerfully and followed him, then turned and smiled
from the water fountain while the group finished their song. I felt
like an idiot. I knew a few of the mothers and their children, and
they smiled sympathetically, but I avoided the faces of the
women I didn't know. When the circle broke up I overheard one
say to another, "What's the *deal?*"

After circle time, it was outside time, but Matthew stood stub-
bornly at the drinking fountain, feeling the water run through his
fingers and watching intently as it went down the drain.

"It's outside time, Matthew," said Gretchen. She pulled him
gently out the door, shutting it behind her. Within moments he
found the outside water fountain.

"Don't worry," she said. "It's an anxious time for him. We'll
give him some time, he'll move on." She was so calm, so serene.
I couldn't remember the last time I had felt calm.

"You go on," she said. "We'll be fine."

"Goodbye, Matthew," I said.

"Goodbye, Matthew," he replied, his eyes on the water flowing
through his fingers.

"Look at Mommy," I said, and he looked up briefly, then

looked down again.

Once again, my mother's car was parked in my driveway at just the right time. The smell of coffee greeted me as I walked through the front door, and Mom was emptying the dishwasher. I told her about the welcome song and the drinking fountain. As I retold it, it sounded so comical that we both started laughing.

"I know you are worried, Laura," Mom said when our laughter subsided. "I worry, too. But don't you remember Eddie Evans from your kindergarten class? Remember how he used to hide under the piano the entire morning? And now he's married and has a family. I think he's got some big job, too."

"I wonder how Eddie Evans's mother is doing," I laughed. "Maybe I'll give her a call. Maybe she can give me some pointers."

"One more thing, Laura," Mom said. "You're getting a little nutty about all this therapy stuff, and that's good, I guess. But you seem almost afraid of Matthew, and he's going to pick up on that if you're not careful."

Mom was right.

From now on, just treat him like there is nothing wrong.

Three hours flew by with the gift of my mother's company, and I returned to Merriewood preschool with anticipation.

"How was your first day of freedom?" asked one friendly face as I looked anxiously for Matthew. "I hope you did something nice for yourself!" Before I could respond, I heard an anxious woman's voice call out to me.

"Are you Matthew Shumaker's mother?"

I looked up and saw an angry woman walking toward me, holding the hand of her crying daughter. *Uh-oh.*

"Gretchen wants to talk to you. I understand Matthew bit my daughter today. Look," she said, thrusting the girl's hand before me. I saw the teeth marks, and a little bit of blood. "We're on our way to the pediatrician."

"I am so sorry," I called out to her, as the friendly faces that had surrounded me earlier scattered. And there stood Matthew, waiting at the gate, with a dreamy smile on his face.

"He had a good day," said Gretchen. "He really did. Then during closing circle time, he just bolted impulsively for Caitlin and bit her hand. I can't explain it."

I looked down at Matthew, biting my lip as tears spilled from my eyes.

"It's his first day," Gretchen said. "Give him some time."

But he didn't have time. He had to catch up.

CHAPTER 11

DESPERATE

MATTHEW WAS ALWAYS IN THE SAME SPOT when I came to pick him up from Merriewood, shoving pieces of tan bark from the play area through the chicken-wire gate at the school entrance. No matter what the weather, his handsome face and blond bangs peeked out from his blue corduroy hooded jacket, and his rosy mouth curved in a slight smile. He was always alone.

"Someone has been looking for you," Gretchen would say, and while Matthew looked happy to see me, it was only because I arrived on time. If I had arrived even five minutes earlier, he would have flipped out and forced me to wait by the gate while he did his bark-shoving. This was just one of the many rituals Matthew insisted on during his day, and he was collecting more all the time.

The group of mothers whom I met at Merriewood were kind to me and to Matthew, and they had included us in a few group playdates. I loved the idea of being included, but the differences between Matthew and the other children his age were amplified when we gathered. I chased Matthew around cheerfully and tried to draw him into the group, but ended up apologizing for his quirks.

"Oops, Matthew, the cookie doesn't go in the heater vent!"

"That's right, Matthew, light! He's fascinated with lights."

"I'm sorry. . . "

In the end, I felt like the manic cheerleader who kept missing her flips.

While I was trying to move Matthew along with Dr. Davies's suggestions, I was haunted by a leaflet I had picked up in her office, one that listed autistic symptoms. It seemed that so many of the items on the list were sprouting in Matthew every day. Those that worried me the most were the ones that had nothing to do with speech and language.

"Insistence on sameness; resists changes in routine."

I have to go around the block before pulling in the driveway or he'll flip out.

"Difficulty mixing with others."

Difficult? He just won't do it.

"Sustained odd play."

The wheels, the drains, lining up toys, licking everything.

I watched the children who were receiving speech therapy getting better, and I resented Matthew because his gains were so much less impressive.

"Wow, Nickie is doing so well," I commented to his mother in the speech waiting room.

"He's made great strides," she replied proudly. "His developmental pediatrician said that he's never seen such a huge improvement in such a short time."

"You're going to a developmental pediatrician? No one told me to see a developmental pediatrician. Who do you go to?

What's their number? What else are you doing? Hold on, let me write this down," I said, digging frantically in my purse.

"You're doing vision therapy, too, aren't you?" she asked. "And you've got to get all the wheat and dairy out of his diet."

I wrote it all down on the back of a grocery receipt.

"How did you hear about all of this stuff?" I asked, feeling like I'd missed out on membership at an exclusive club.

"From other parents, mostly," she said. "But if I were you, I'd get on the developmental pediatrician's list right away. Matthew's autistic, right?"

She threw it out just like that. I felt the blood rush to my face and my heart raced dangerously.

"I don't, we don't know yet," I managed. I wanted to hide, to disappear.

"I just assumed," said the mother. "Gosh, I'm sorry. I'm sure he'll be fine."

Again, I spied at Matthew from the rearview window as we drove home, and I wondered. When was the last time I looked at him and smiled proudly? When was the last time I didn't suspect that there was anything wrong?

I needed to remember. I needed to get that feeling back, or I would go crazy.

CHAPTER 12

THE PSYCHOLOGIST'S PERSPECTIVE

IT TOOK ME OVER AN HOUR during a cold December rainstorm to get to Brian Hoffman's office near Stanford University. Matthew studied the windshield wipers during the drive, and Andy slept. When Dr. Hoffman greeted us in the waiting room that he shared with two other therapists, my eyes filled with tears, and the ordeal of getting there was immediately forgotten.

Dr. Hoffman's redwood-paneled office was tidy but warm with a big leather couch and chairs. A bookcase contained a mix of professional books and manuals, child development tomes, and children's stories. In the corner was a play table that converted into a sandbox.

We spent just a few minutes getting reacquainted, and then Dr. Hoffman took Matthew's hand.

"Let's do some drawing, Matthew," he said. "Your mom and Andy are going for a walk. They'll be right back."

"Right back," said Matthew, still echolalic despite months of speech therapy.

"We'll see you in about an hour," Dr. Hoffman said, closing the door behind him.

———————

"What do you think?" I asked the doctor anxiously when I returned. "Do you think it's serious? Do you think it's autism? Or something else? And if it is autism, is there some way we can turn things around?"

Dr. Hoffman told me that Matthew did display many autistic traits, but that it would be premature to diagnose him just yet.

"He may have been traumatized by an event in the family, such as Andy's birth, which caused him to withdraw," he said while watching the two brothers play side by side.

"Could it be something I did? Or Peter? Maybe a babysitter that was mean to him?"

I started to cry.

"I am not saying that anyone did anything. It may just be that Matthew is a sensitive child, and that he has reacted to normal family events by withdrawing. If that is the case, play therapy could help draw him out."

He proposed two sessions a week for Matthew, and monthly parent appointments to discuss Matthew's progress.

Wow, that's gotta be expensive! And an hour drive each way!

———————

I drove home in turmoil. This would be a big commitment. But I knew that Dr. Hoffman wouldn't suggest it unless he believed it would help. He's the expert.

But they're all experts. Who do I believe?

Maybe insurance will cover this. Maybe my parents will help.

How would I do it?

Preschool Monday, Wednesday, and Friday. That's when I'll work. Then when I pick him up from school, we'll run to speech therapy. Tuesday and Thursday will be Dr. Hoffman's days. I'll keep Andy up until it's time to go and he can nap in the car. Maybe I'll have to quit my job. Can we afford it?

When I went over Dr. Hoffman's theory with Peter, he grew pale.

"You've got to be kidding! Traumatized? Give me a break!"

"The way he explained it was, some children are more sensitive than others and react to regular things by withdrawing." I struggled to explain what Dr. Hoffman had told me today, and finally gave up. I had to admit it sounded like psychobabble, but I needed to trust someone.

"Just call him and get it all from him," I said, throwing up my hands. I was exhausted, utterly confused, and scared.

"I'll call him," Peter said, "but there is no way we're going to do this. Can't you find anyone closer?"

"Peter," I said, crazed, "I just can't go to another doctor, answer all the same questions in another freaky office, and put Matthew through it—again!"

My parents came over for dinner that evening, and the four of us churned over all of the advice we had heard since Matthew's first evaluation less than six months before.

"All I want," said Peter, "is for one person, one expert, to say 'Here is what is wrong with Matthew, and here is exactly what you should do.'"

"It seems that you would be smart to try everything within

reason," said my dad, "and step back and see what's working. And by the way, just raise your hand if you need help with this. We mean it. And I'm sure your parents would do the same."

I looked at my mom, who was gazing out the window at Matthew while he played with the garden hose. She seemed so sad.

"I wonder what he's thinking about," she said. "I wonder if he knows we're worried about him."

CHAPTER 13

THE FOLLOW-UP

WANTING TO LEAVE NO STONE UNTURNED, I followed the advice of the presumptuous mother in the speech therapy waiting room and scheduled Matthew for an evaluation with a developmental pediatrician just a few weeks after our initial meeting with Dr. Hoffman.

"Isn't this overkill?" asked Peter. "He was just tested by Dr. Hoffman. All this testing has got to confuse the poor kid."

"But a developmental pediatrician will look at Matthew's development from a medical perspective and make referrals to other specialists if needed," I said, though I agreed that it was a little ridiculous to test him again so soon.

After testing Matthew, the developmental pediatrician started by giving us the most encouraging news of all. "Many areas of his delay are quite mild," he said, "and Matthew has splinter skills, which are areas where he is at or *above* age level. With continued focus on speech and language, I'm optimistic about Matthew's prognosis."

Peter and I looked at each other and pumped our fists. Good news!

"This is wonderful!" I exclaimed.

"The fact that a significant delay exists is evident," the doctor hedged.

Uh-oh.

He took out a pad of paper and a pen and sketched an arc.

"This arc represents a scale," he said, making a small mark at the bottom of the scale. "This is where Matthew scores on the Stanford-Binet Intelligence Scale."

I stared at the drawing, not comprehending what the doctor was trying to tell us.

"That looks low," said Peter.

"He is in the second percentile," the doctor replied.

"That'll change once the language improves, right?" I asked.

"No, this is an actual measure of Matthew's cognitive ability," he said, still pointing at the two-percentile mark with his fancy pen.

"But you said we should be optimistic. You said he had splinter skills. And he is now seeing a psychologist twice a week for play therapy. Don't you think that maybe it all just hasn't clicked yet?"

"I don't have a crystal ball," he said, "but Matthew is in an optimal spot at the moment. It would also be in his best interest for you to consult your local school district about placement in special-education classes. You should also contact the Regional Center of the East Bay. They provide services for children with developmental disabilities and their families."

"Wait a minute," I started, but Peter held up his hand to silence me.

"Just so we're clear," he said. "You say that Matthew has

made substantial growth in all areas. But when I look at this scale, it looks like he's retarded."

"Dr. Davies said he *wasn't* retarded," I broke in, "and he doesn't *look* retarded. He just doesn't test well. Dr. Hoffman is going to draw him out—"

"Lau-*ra*," Peter said, trying to calm me.

"OK," I said, jumping up, "we'll talk to the school district *and* the regional. . . whatever, but you know what? I'm kind of upset. We can talk more about this another time."

Peter and the doctor sat frozen in their chairs. They looked afraid of me.

I gathered up my purse and my blank notepad and rushed out. Peter followed me to the car, where I was pacing angrily.

"Let's walk around the block," I said, shaking. "I've got to move."

Peter tried to take my hand, but I refused it.

"I know, Laura, this is a big blow."

"No, it's not! He's got it wrong! The problem is that all these people have such different ideas about what's going on with Matthew and it's making me insane! First, it wasn't autism or retardation, then I get used to the idea that it might be autism, but *good news*! Dr. Hoffman thinks he can draw him out of it. And now this guy says he's a retard!" I started to laugh, a crazy, stress-driven laugh headed toward hysterical tears.

"I know, Laura," said Peter. "It's so bad, it's almost funny."

"And one last thing," I said once I had pulled myself together. "I will hurt the next one of them that uses that 'crystal ball' line."

CHAPTER 14

KINDERGARTEN

THREE MONTHS LATER, I stood in the dressing room of Gap Kids with Matthew and Andy, clothes heaped all around us, trying to find just the right outfit for Matthew's first day of kindergarten. Matthew squirmed and laughed as I wrestled shirts and shorts over his busy body. When he dove under the door of the fitting room dressed only in his Batman underpants, I grabbed him by the leg and pulled him back in before he made a scene. But the shopping trip was over.

"I think the red shirt looks neat," said Andy. "Can we go now?"

Andy had been an amiable two-year-old when family preoccupations switched abruptly from Halloween costumes to what to do about Matthew. He took walks with me while his big brother was in speech therapy and broke the silence of a droning car ride to the child psychologist with "Well, it's a beautiful day today, isn't it?"

His favorite outfit was a pair of khaki corduroy pants, a turtleneck with bears around the collar and down the sleeves, and a pair of shoes with cars on them—a miniature man who spoke in full sentences.

"How *old* is he?" astonished passersby would ask when they overheard him conversing with me on our walks.

Now, at three, he was already a skilled mediator.

Any woman in her right mind would not go shopping with two boys, aged three and five, but I was a woman on the edge, having learned just days before that what I'd feared and suspected was true. Matthew was autistic. The official diagnosis of autism came from another specialist who was a colleague of Dr. Hoffman's.

"Back-to-school shopping, eh?" asked the saleslady, handing me my bag. "Where do your kids go?"

I felt my face flush. "The little one goes to preschool at Merriewood, and Matthew goes to Burton Valley. He'll be in kindergarten."

"You're kidding! My daughter starts there too! She got Mrs. Miller. How about your son?"

"He's in the special class with Miss Adams."

"The special class?" said the saleslady competitively. "I thought the gifted class didn't start till the second grade."

"The special class for kids with learning disabilities," I clarified.

"*Ohhh*," she said, coolly examining Matthew, who was now licking the mirror next to the register. "Bless his heart. Bless *your* heart, for that matter!"

While we had suspected for some time that it was autism, the news still leveled us and made us question whether we were doing the right things. Was I wasting my time driving back and forth to psychologists and speech therapists, time that could be spent doing something more effective? And what *was* the right thing?

There had been a lot of talk about the Lovaas early intervention program for children with autism. It was a behavior modification program designed to enhance the development of communication skills and represented a huge commitment involving forty hours a week of intensive one-on-one therapy with trained tutors. I had heard reports, however, that it had helped some children totally recover from autism. Should I seriously consider this?

"Matthew is too old for the program," said the new specialist, "and too high-functioning. The program is most successful with children up to three and a half years, before stereotypical and disruptive behaviors become established. And," she added, "there is no cure for autism."

I believed that the psychologist was making progress with Matthew, but Peter wasn't so sure.

"A woman in my office has a friend whose cousin is autistic," Peter told me, glancing at Dr. Hoffman's latest bill, "and she said psychotherapy doesn't work for autistic people."

"Not all people with autism are alike, Peter, and we don't know anything about the cousin's case." I started crying. I fell apart easily these days.

"Dr. Hoffman has been helping Matthew a *lot*," I wept. "He is talking more and is communicating his feelings better."

The most helpful aspect of Matthew's visits with Dr. Hoffman was what I was learning about Matthew and his autistic brain. I was particularly curious about Matthew's rituals and his insistence on sameness.

"Matthew's internal world is very confusing," Dr. Hoffman

explained. "He depends on routine and rituals to restore order."

"What about his random, impulsive behavior?" I asked the doctor. "Why does he bite kids in his class, apparently out of the blue? Why does he throw toys and rocks at other children—and then *laugh?*"

He explained that Matthew's impulsive ways were his attempt to connect with people. When he bites someone or throws a toy at them, he gets a reaction, albeit a negative one. Dr. Hoffman would work on helping Matthew communicate appropriately, with language.

On Matthew's first day of school, I dressed him in his new red shirt and blue shorts and white Velcro shoes. I combed his hair and took a picture of him for the scrapbook, hoping that someday I could say, "This picture was taken on your first day of kindergarten, just months before we cured you of autism!" His expression in the picture wasn't happy or sad but passive, like a man waiting in line at the bank.

I arrived at Matthew's classroom fifteen minutes early, hoping that I could watch his new classmates arrive with their mothers. I had been feeling *so* isolated and was anxious to connect with these women who, like me, had been through so much.

But Matthew and I walked into a full classroom, with no mothers in sight.

"Good morning, Matthew!" said Miss Adams, Matthew's fresh-faced young teacher. "It's nice to see you again. Come on over and we'll introduce you to your classmates."

There were six children in the class including Matthew—four boys and two girls. None of them, except for the blind boy,

Adam, *looked* disabled as they sat at their desks.

"Are we late?" I asked.

"No, they're early. On the first day, the bus drops the kids off early."

My heart sank.

"They all came on the bus? Even on their first day of kindergarten?"

Miss Adams nodded. "Will Matthew be taking the bus?"

I had great memories of my mom driving me to and from kindergarten. I was always so excited to see her by the classroom door waiting to hear about my day.

"No, I like driving him," I said. "I hoped I could meet some of the moms today. I thought since it was the first day—"

"All of the parents should be at Back to School Night next week," said Miss Adams.

What a bunch of cold women!

I tried to hold back my tears, but I felt so undone—not just because the mothers didn't show up, but by the whole scene.

"You must think I'm a nut!" I said, wiping my tears.

"Mommy cries a lot," Andy confided to Miss Adams, "but she's fine."

"All moms cry on the first day of kindergarten," said Miss Adams, smiling.

"Goodbye, Matthew!" I called from the doorway, but he was already busy with the water fountain. He had recently added a new twist to the water fountain routine. While one hand was under the stream of water, the other was flapping, and he stopped intermittently to jump and dip down to touch the floor, laughing and drooling. Dr. Hoffman told me this was called self-stimulating behavior, and Matthew used it to cope with an over-stimulating environment.

"Is he having a fit?" a mother at the park had asked me over the summer.

"No," I responded. "He's just overwhelmed, and he's working it out."

Once in the car, I put on a smile for Andy.

"Do you want to go see Grandma?" I asked.

"OK," he said, peering up at me. "You're fine now, right, Mommy?"

"I'm better than finc," I said, hugging my insightful, sympathetic three-year-old. "I'm great!"

CHAPTER 15

THE MIRACLE CURE

DURING WINTER BREAK in Matthew's first-grade year, and without the support of the experts who were currently working with Matthew, Peter and I decided to try the miracle cure: Auditory Training.

"Did you see that girl on *Oprah*?" I asked Dr. Hoffman. "I don't usually watch *Oprah*, but one day I flipped it on while I was folding the laundry. Anyway, through this amazing treatment, this girl went from autistic and functionally retarded to gifted."

The theory behind auditory training, simply put, was that some children who suffer from learning and behavioral disorders, including autism, are hypersensitive to certain frequencies of sound. Auditory training was designed to normalize hearing and the ways in which the brain processes auditory information.

"We figured that since Matthew is hypersensitive to sound, auditory training might cure him. Do you know anyone who has tried it?"

Dr. Hoffman had not seen the girl on *Oprah*, but Christy, the speech therapist, said she knew some parents who had tried the training.

"It's very expensive," she added. "Some claim that they have seen some improvement, but none of my clients has been 'cured' by it. There has been no clinical proof that it works, so I'm skeptical."

"Let me put it this way," I said. "If it were your child, would you try it?"

"No."

But Peter and I were already carried away by the wave of information we had gathered on auditory training since the young girl's appearance on the *Oprah* show. What if Matthew's autism was caused by hypersensitivity to sound, and what if this one treatment improved his life forever? And how guilty would we feel if someday, some specialist said, "If only he'd had auditory training when he was six. . . "

"I know that if I heard everything as acutely as Matthew does," Peter said, "I'd have a hard time focusing on anything else. I'd go mad."

Matthew started the training just two weeks after the birth of our third son, John. As soon as it became clear that Matthew's disability would be lifelong, I was desperate to have a third child. "We don't want our boys to be viewed as 'the normal one and the one with the problem,'" I told Peter. "Can you imagine what a burden it would be for Andy down the road?"

Peter agreed with the idea of having a third, but thought we should find out if we were at risk of having another child with autism. The responses from the experts were mixed, and Peter was ambivalent, but I pressed, reasoned, and begged and finally we took a chance. John was the most beautiful of my three babies and appeared normal, but we would have to wait a while to see whether he had escaped autism.

The closest auditory training practitioner we could find was in Marin County, about an hour's drive north on a good day. Peter agreed that he would be in charge of taking Matthew to and from the ten-day program, during which Matthew would listen to music wearing headphones fitted with a special electronic device. The device filtered frequencies from the music, sending modified sounds into Matthew's ears and training his auditory nerve to process sound normally. Each day of the training, Matthew would wear the headphones for thirty minutes in the morning followed by a three-hour break, and thirty minutes in the afternoon.

"Matthew and I can go out for lunch and for a hike between sessions," said Peter. "It will be fun."

The training facilitator suggested that before the training we put headphones on Matthew at home as much as possible to get him used to it.

"And if he doesn't get used to it, don't worry, we can make the headphones so loose that he won't know he has them on. And we have plenty of toys to keep him busy."

"But will the treatment work if the headphones are loose?"

"Oh, don't worry, they won't be *too* loose!"

Even with a two-week-old baby, I went along for the ride the first day of training. The "facilitator," who was also a psychotherapist, had sounded quite professional on the phone, but I wanted to meet her in person. "I work with my husband," she had said. "He is also a therapist, and great with kids."

The husband greeted us when we arrived and ushered us into his office. He was tall and thin and wore a full beard, Birkenstocks, and a leather vest over a paisley shirt.

"It smells like garbage in here," said Matthew. The husband opened a window.

The office reminded me of a low-rent version of Dr. Hoffman's.

Instead of a sleek, leather chair there was a beat-up brown recliner, and next to it a large beanbag chair with toys strewn all around it. I looked at the certificate on the wall.

"You do hypnotherapy, too?" I asked, and he nodded.

"That's my bread and butter. My wife will give Matthew an audiogram before we start, another during the middle of treatment, and then a final one when treatment has been completed. We'll make adjustments to the filter along the way to get the best result. You should see some results immediately following the last treatment, but the full effect won't be apparent until six months after the treatment is completed."

"Do you guarantee your work?" asked Peter.

"Yes. After the six-month period, we'll do another audiogram and more treatment if he needs it."

If you're still here in six months.

"Can I see the headphones?" I asked. "I'd just like to see how they fit Matthew."

The husband sat Matthew in the beanbag chair and put the headphones on him. Then he turned on the music and Matthew started laughing—a crazy, scary laugh.

"See?" said Peter. "He likes it."

I knew what Peter was thinking. We have already put $1500 into this thing, fifty percent of the total, and damn it, it's gonna work.

"Where *is* your wife?" Peter asked, and a red-headed beauty wearing a gauzy peasant dress came floating in breathlessly.

"Sorry I'm late," she said. "My cat is sick."

Yeah, well I've got a two-week-old baby, and I'm early.

"Do you have any questions?" she asked.

The husband had answered our questions, so we said no.

Peter and I took our seats in the waiting room. Baby John slept, and Andy opened his new coloring book. I glanced through the vertical blinds into the room where the wife was giving Matthew his audiogram, the husband by her side looking befuddled.

"Peter?" I whispered. "Look."

"Oh, man," he sighed. "If *this* pair cures Matthew, *that* would be the miracle."

———————

Peter and I studied Matthew carefully once he had completed the training, watching for his reaction to sounds and for any improvement in his behavior.

"I think he's little better," said Peter one evening as the family sat down to dinner. Then as if on cue, Matthew jumped up from the table and ran outside. We followed him and found him smiling intensely as he looked skyward at the white trail of an airplane. Then he jumped up and down, laughing and drooling, his hands flapping.

"They said we might not see the full effect for six months," Peter said as I shook my head.

"Yeah, we'll have to mark that on the calendar."

———————

Any improvements that were gained by auditory training, real or imagined, were erased in an instant on the third Monday of Matthew's second-grade year, two months after the magical six-month deadline. Someone pulled the school fire alarm, and Matthew refused to take his hands off his ears—for three whole months. A special meeting was called at school; even Dr. Hoffman attended, but no one was able to get Matthew to take his hands off his ears.

Finally, Matthew's grandpa surprised him at school one morning, took Matthew's wrists and said, "Matthew. It's safe now."

And that was that.

NAVIGATING
CHILDHOOD

CHAPTER 16

BROTHERS

"I WONDER WHAT IT WOULD BE LIKE to have a big brother?" five-year-old Andy asked me. We were taking one of our walks around the Stanford campus while Matthew was in therapy with Dr. Hoffman. He wasn't being reflective. He was being realistic.

Andy had become the big brother during an outing to the park two years before, when he was three and Matthew five.

A boy whom Andy had befriended that day approached Matthew. Matthew called the boy a rock head. Incensed, the boy confronted Andy.

"Your brother called me a rock head!" he protested.

"Oh, don't worry," Andy replied reassuringly. "That's just his natural way of talking. My mom has some juice. Would you like some?"

Will it always be this easy?

A little over a year after the rock head incident, John was born.

It's remarkable how soon you can tell that your baby is developmentally healthy after having had one who is not. It was clear to Peter and me that John was making the right connections from an early age. Once he started to talk at age two, I tested him for echolalia.

"What did you do at school today, John? Did you read a book?"

"Yes, and I played in the sand. How are you, Mom?"

"Fine! Did you have a snack?"

"I had goldfish and juice. I love you, Mommy."

Matthew at the same age would have answered "Read a book" and "Have a snack," while lining up his blocks, inspecting the wheels on his toy truck, or watching water go down a drain, glancing at me for just a second.

I also made sure John's eyes met mine when I talked with him, and watched for any sign of the repetitive, ritualistic behaviors we remembered from Matthew's early days.

John was a blessing to Andy, whose first friend was growing increasingly remote. By age six and a half, Matthew, more than ever, preferred playing alone. He'd line up his toys and make towers with his blocks until they toppled over, again and again, or swing gleefully on the backyard swing. During John's first year, Matthew picked up a disturbing new quirk of running to the toddler's side when he was crying, and jumping up and down with excitement. He did the same when Andy was distressed or angry. It kept the entire family on edge.

As the years went by, Andy thrived in spite of his brother's increasing strangeness. In one family movie, five-year-old Andy is reading haltingly to John in a big white rocking chair. Matthew is sitting on the floor behind the rocking chair, watching the shadows left by the chair as it rocks to and fro, his hands flapping with the movement.

Because John was nearly seven years younger than Matthew, it would be a while before he noticed his brother's unusual behavior. Andy was aware of Matthew's disability, but it didn't seem to bother him—until he entered the first grade.

That was the first year Matthew and Andy attended the same school. In September, I signed up to drive for Andy's field trip to the Jelly Belly Factory. I was driving along blissfully in my minivan full of six-year-olds when I heard whispering and snickering from the backseat. Andy was behind me; I could see his hazel eyes in the rearview mirror, glistening with tears, his chin trembling. He was not easily shaken.

"What's going on, guys?" I asked.

"Andy's brother is a retard!" a brave soul blurted out, and laughter erupted. Who in the hell did they think was driving the car?

With a very large lump in my throat and blood rushing to my face, I thought it would be wise to pull over and straighten things out.

The car fell deadly silent as I pulled over. When I turned around, Andy was looking down at his knees, mortified, while the boys struggled to wipe off their smirks and look somber. I had no idea what to say, so I decided not to try to stick up for Matthew just yet.

"Should I turn the car around and take everyone to the principal's office?" I threatened.

"Joey said it!" three boys exclaimed at once. Andy glanced up at me with a slight smile.

My look of disapproval was punishment enough, and we continued on our way.

The thirty-five-minute drive was very quiet. I turned on music and chattered like an idiot the whole time. When we got to the jellybean factory, all the boys, except for Andy, bolted to join the rest of the class. I told the teacher I needed a minute with Andy.

What should I say? But Andy took the initiative.

"Mom, we're going to have to think of a way to explain things for the next time this happens," he said earnestly. I hugged him tight, and his small hand patted my back, my sweet boy comforting me in return. But all of a sudden I felt the weight of what was to come, the comments, the teasing, the brave explanations, the heartache. I felt such tremendous sadness for Andy, and for myself.

Later that day, I relayed the events of the day to my dad, who stopped by after visiting a client in our area. Andy came running to the sound of his grandpa's booming voice.

"Your mom was telling me it was a tough day, but you look pretty happy to me!" he said, smiling.

Andy beamed. "Did you come here just to see *me*?" he asked.

"Yep. Now go jump in my car before your brothers find out," and off they went for an ice cream cone, Matthew's big brother and his grandpa.

CHAPTER 17

LIVING WITH THE LOOKS

IT WAS NOT YET THREE YEARS since the word autism had first been used in diagnosing Matthew.

Peter and I sat at the kitchen table adding up all of the hours Matthew had spent since then in therapy, testing, and treatment.

"So, roughly 108 hours of speech therapy, and 196 hours of play therapy," said Peter.

"No, we cut Dr. Hoffman down to once a week seven months ago," I said. "So, more like 152 hours. Let's not forget about auditory training."

"What about the diet thing?" asked Peter.

We had met other parents with autistic children who had removed gluten and dairy from their children's diets and noticed a dramatic improvement in behavior.

"Studies show that some people with autism have trouble digesting certain proteins," said the parents, "and then too many peptides are absorbed, disrupting biochemistry and brain function."

Makes sense.

I had tried removing wheat and dairy from Matthew's diet a

year before, when he was seven, but gave up when his already-thin body dropped much-needed weight.

"I don't think I have the energy to try it again right now," I told Peter. Just talking about all we had done—and hadn't—was wearing me out.

"Let's take a break," I sighed. "You should do something just with Andy and John today."

We were reevaluating our course after a difficult family outing to the museum the day before. It had ended badly when Matthew saw an elderly woman trip and fall. He ran to her side, jumped up and down, and laughed as if he had seen a clown's stunt at the circus. Onlookers were appalled as we dragged our seven-year-old son from the museum. John smiled, oblivious in his stroller, but Andy followed us, downcast, his chin quivering.

"I'm so sorry," I said, holding Andy.

"It's not your fault," he gulped. "He does those things because of his brain problem."

Compensatory outings almost made Matthew's scenes worthwhile, and Andy and John counted on them.

My morning with Matthew had started out well. We cooked breakfast together and then got out the watercolors and did some painting. After about an hour, Matthew and I went to the grocery store where he behaved beautifully. But when we went to check out, he leaned over and licked the conveyer belt that moves the groceries to the checker. I heard the bag boy snicker and the woman behind me in line gasp.

It didn't seem the right time to explain that my son liked to lick things because he had sensory issues.

"No, Matthew," I said, and he fell on his back, laughing and squirming. I desperately grabbed a bag of Skittles and tried to bribe him to his feet.

"Who's in charge here?" The voice came from the well-coiffed, sixtyish woman who stood behind us in line. By the time my groceries were bagged and I headed toward the exit, I heard her confide to the clerk, "She ought to teach him. . . " I left the store with a pleasant look on my face, then burst into tears once in my car.

"Stop crying!" yelled Matthew. "Be happy. Laugh!"

I stifled my tears and let out a fake laugh to subdue him. I really needed to cry, but I knew my best chance was to get home and settle Matthew on the couch with a Raffi video. I could then sneak off to the bathroom, turn on the water, and let loose.

The looks and the snickering had become a way of life now that Matthew's ability to blend in had faded. He stood too close to people and asked strange questions.

"How many airports have you been to?"

"Why do you smell bad?"

Or to an Asian: "You should work at China Palace."

I understood that Matthew's strange questions were his attempt to connect with people, but I couldn't explain this to everyone in the heat of the moment. I didn't worry so much about the laughter, but about preserving Matthew's dignity, and I did whatever I could to remove him from embarrassing public situations, even if it meant bribery with Skittles. I had given up thinking about how I might look, and I knew people stared and talked about us. I heard comments like "She's a saint!" or "Poor thing" or "She ought to leave him home!"

Well-meaning friends watched me struggle with him and pointed out that God wouldn't give me more than I could handle. "Your other two boys will be better people for having a brother like Matthew," some would say. "You think *you* have it bad, I know someone who has twins with autism, a child with cancer, a brother with cerebral palsy. . . "

Did I ever say I had it bad? And why should the misfortunes of others make me feel better?

Peter returned home with an exhilarated Andy and a sleeping John.

"We walked all the way across the Golden Gate Bridge and then took a cable car!" said Andy. "Where's Matthew? We got him something," and he ran off to find him.

"Thank you so much, Laura," said Peter. "We had a great time. How did things go here?"

"They went great," I lied. No one likes a killjoy. "But I think I'll get out and go for a walk or something."

"You look tired. *Really* tired," said Peter. "Why don't you take a nap first?"

"Thanks, I think I will," I said, taking two steps to the sofa, where clean laundry was piled, waiting to be folded. I shoved it out of the way just enough to collapse in a heap for a deep, much-needed sleep.

CHAPTER 18

THE BABYSITTER

"MOM?" asked Matthew. "Where is the closest airport?"

"Oakland," I answered with a sigh.

"Where is the next airport?"

"San Francisco. Then San Jose, Morgan Hill. . . "

"Stop! I need to ask you first," Matthew wailed.

This new obsession about airports was wearing me out. I was only allowed to stop answering him when the phone or the doorbell interrupted us.

It was the second week of the following summer, and I was already wondering how I could stay sane until September. But I heaved a sigh of relief when I learned that Rocky was looking for a summer job.

Rocky, the fourteen-year-old son of Matthew's old preschool teacher, had been babysitting for us for the past year. He was a great kid from a loving Mormon family who was too good to be true. He handled Matthew's odd behavior with good humor and was loved by all three of my boys. I knew that if he were in a pickle, he could call his mom for advice or rescue, but he never needed to. He often watched the boys at his house—a dream home with a trampoline and a game room filled with arcade machines.

Rocky agreed to babysit three mornings a week and an occasional Saturday night. When I told my parents about the arrangement, they were thrilled and insisted on paying Rocky themselves.

"Just knowing that you're getting a break gives us great peace of mind," said my dad, joking that the money would come out of my inheritance.

But Rocky wasn't available on the one night that we really needed the help.

Peter had left his sales job at IBM, where he'd worked since we were married, and he was now managing a computer services company. He was hosting a dinner in San Francisco for some clients, and we had to secure a sitter.

Three boys between the ages of two and eight is a tall babysitting order under normal circumstances, but with Matthew in the mix, it was a tremendous challenge finding help.

I called my brother Scott, who lived in a nearby town with his wife Vicki and their three kids. Scott was a lot like my dad and was great with Matthew. But no luck—they would be away that weekend.

"Try your parents," suggested Peter.

"Sweetheart, we'd love to," said Dad, "but your mama isn't feeling her best. We're just waiting to hear from her doctor."

"Oh, my God! What's wrong?"

"Don't worry, Laura. She's just a little out of breath. It's probably just her asthma acting up. She'll lay low and be as good as new tomorrow. I'll put her on and she'll reassure you."

"Hi, Laura," said Mom. "I am *fine*. Don't worry. I might just need a little antibiotic or something. Promise you won't worry or *I'll* worry!" she joked.

Desperate, and now worried about my mother's health, I decided to call Rocky's mom, Laurie. With her preschool connections, she might know someone who could handle our crew.

"What about Anna?" she asked.

Anna, Laurie said, was a friend who had just moved from England to be a nanny for a family in our community. She had worked at a school for disabled children back home and was looking for work on her days off.

Jackpot! I thanked Laurie and assured her that Rocky would always be first choice. Then I phoned Anna and explained our situation. Responding enthusiastically, she told me about her exceptional qualifications, which included a special-education teaching credential and CPR certification. She had decided to take a year off to be a nanny in the U.S. and was interested in finding babysitting jobs on the weekends. I immediately had fantasies of a weekend away, which we badly needed, while this perfect person took care of the kids.

Saturday arrived, and I was running around the house with a Windex bottle preparing for Anna. I had a theory that when the house is clean, babysitters are nicer to the kids. Matthew had been throwing Andy's Ninja turtles over the fence, and Peter was about to embark on a discussion of consequences when the doorbell rang.

"Anna! Come on in!" I said, knowing immediately as she

appeared before us that we might have a problem here.

Anna had a big smile, beautiful blue eyes, dangly earrings—and a hundred extra pounds.

Matthew came to the door and got right down to business.

"How big are you?"

"*Matthew!*" I gasped, horrified, but not surprised.

Anna seemed unfazed. "Hello, Matthew! I'm Anna! Would you like to show me your room?"

By now, Andy and John were standing behind me, looking worried and knowing what was to come.

"How big are you?" Matthew repeated. I was about to jump in again when Anna signaled to me that she could handle it.

"I am a bit chubby, I suppose."

"How fat arc you?" Matthew persisted.

Why didn't Laurie tell me?

"In England, we call it chubby, so I guess you would say I'm quite chubby!"

"So, you're big and fat," Matthew concluded calmly.

"Could you excuse me a minute, Anna?" I said, taking Matthew's hand.

Peter appeared, and introductions were made.

"Will you give Anna a little tour? I need to talk to Matthew for a minute."

Wide-eyed like the boys, Peter walked off with Anna as I walked Matthew to his room.

"She must eat a lot of food," Matthew said to me while Anna was still within earshot.

"Matthew," I said, shutting his door, "I don't want you to talk about how fat Anna is anymore. It hurts her feelings."

"But she is fat," he said flatly.

"I know, and she knows it too, but it isn't nice to talk about people's appearance."

"What does 'appearance' mean?" he asked.

"It means it is not nice to talk about what people look like." I paused. How could I get this concept through to him? "What if someone said, 'Matthew, you're ugly' or 'Matthew, you're too skinny.' Wouldn't that hurt your feelings?"

"No."

I could see that I would not be able to fix this right away, so I took a shortcut. "Matthew. Here is the rule. You will not talk about how fat Anna is. If you can follow that rule, then I'll buy you a special balloon tomorrow."

"OK," said Matthew, smiling.

Peter knocked on the door.

"We've got to get going," he said. "Matthew, be nice, OK?"

"Get me a shiny balloon," Matthew said as I went out to face Anna.

"I am so sorry," I told Anna, wondering if I should call the whole thing off. The weekend getaway of my dreams would have to wait.

"Don't worry! The little ones always comment on my size, but once they get over it, we have a jolly old time!" But I knew Matthew wouldn't get over it, and that it was going to be a *long* evening for poor Anna.

I had a hard time relaxing and getting in the spirit of the dinner party, but I finally shared our story with a few of the guests, who laughed uproariously.

"When did you find out he was autistic?" one of them asked.

"I hear they're brilliant," said another.

"What will he be like when he's a man?"

We snuck out of the dinner early and joked uneasily about what might be going on at home.

Back at the house, Anna looked ragged and relieved to see us.

"How'd it go?" I asked cautiously.

"Anna ate pizza and ice cream," Matthew reported.

I quickly ushered Anna out to her car and folded a big check into her hand.

"I don't know how you do it!" she said with a dazed smile.

I thanked her and said I hoped she would come again. What else was I going to say? He hadn't meant to, but Matthew had hurt this woman, and I felt terrible.

"Matthew," I sighed as I walked back inside. "I thought you weren't going to talk about how big Anna was."

"I didn't. I just told her she shouldn't eat so much."

"Matthew," Peter jumped in, "let's go through this one more time."

"Thank you," I mouthed to Peter, my hand over my heart as the two walked back to Matthew's room.

Peter emerged from Matthew's room twenty minutes later, shaking his head.

"He just doesn't get it!" said my exasperated husband. "Maybe you should have Dr. Hoffman work on this. Maybe this 'drawing Matthew out' business needs some fine-tuning."

I lay in bed that night with thoughts buzzing.

Should I get him the balloon? At least he's talking. I wonder how Mom is. Should I write Anna a note? What if Mom has cancer or something? I wonder if I'm spending enough time with Andy and John. Did I water the roses today?

On and on. And then it was morning.

CHAPTER 19

FINDING HELP

IT WAS AFTER A PUBLIC ANXIETY ATTACK at California Pizza Kitchen, where our family of five was celebrating my birthday about a week after the babysitting fiasco, that I came to the inevitable conclusion: I needed to find my own therapist.

That night, Peter and I had just suffered through a particularly grueling meeting at Matthew's school, where he was now in the fourth grade. One of the behavior specialists had come up with the idea of polling Matthew's peers, the regular-education kids that he was mainstreamed with at recess, and asking what they thought of him.

"He's weird."

"He smells bad."

"I'm scared of him."

These were just a few of the responses that sent me crying from the IEP (Individual Education Plan) meeting in tears.

That behavior specialist didn't last in the district very long.

When we arrived at the restaurant, my eyes were still swollen from crying. Peter thought that a family dinner at a kid-friendly place would be a great way to cheer me up.

The restaurant was surrounded by shops in an outdoor mall, and as we took our seats I soon found myself overwhelmed by the crowds streaming around inside and out, by the din of their voices—by everything. With the five of us crammed around a table for four, I remember looking across at Matthew—his blond hair shining under the glaring lights, his beautiful brown eyes not meeting mine, his distracted smile—and feeling a crushing heaviness in my heart, too acute to share with anyone. He wore a red polo shirt, one I had picked out; it made him easy to spot in a crowd should he dash away impulsively, as he was known to do.

Sitting anxiously at the small table, my knees jammed against its legs, I suddenly felt the shock of a spoon hitting me in the chest, hurled by Matthew as he darted out of the restaurant giggling into the sea of people. Up and out of the restaurant I flew, tackling Matthew to the pavement as he was about to dart into a busy street, surrounded by the judging eyes of onlookers. Sobbing, breathless, and utterly depleted, I couldn't see daylight. I dreaded my future.

I had always been a healthy person, but lately every cold I caught turned into bronchitis or worse. Stomach pains and sleepless nights stretched on for days. I knew Peter and my parents worried about me, but I was beyond their ability to help. I fretted about the expense of seeking professional help for myself, about whether all funds should be devoted to Matthew's cause, and wondered if I would be able to find a therapist who could connect with me and help me bear the weight of my uncertain future.

I hadn't had great luck with therapists in the past. The first time I saw a therapist, I was a few years out of college and needed direction. I chose a radio psychologist who told me as soon as I sat down that she was going through a difficult divorce, and that she was waiting for an important call that she would have to take. While waiting for the call, she told me of all the famous people she had met in her role as a radio personality.

The next one I found told me I had a self-esteem problem as a result of having recently been dumped by a boyfriend. She asked me to role-play with an empty chair.

"Tell Charlie how you are feeling. Go ahead and hit him if you're angry." I think I actually yelled at the chair, but refrained from hitting it.

When Andy was a baby and we were beginning to worry about Matthew, Peter and I went to a therapist to talk about our struggles with balancing marriage and a growing family. His name was Roger Glum, of all things, and he had an annoying habit of looking at Peter while I talked, and then at me when Peter spoke.

After gauging our reaction toward one another, he paused and asked, "Do you guys watch *thirtysomething?*"

Yes, we had seen *thirtysomething*, a TV show filmed in muted tones about whiny couples also struggling to balance marriage and growing families. So?

———

I asked my doctor for a referral, and he enthusiastically recommended Rebecca Elliott.

The day of my first appointment with Dr. Elliott, I almost backed out. What could anyone say to me to help me with my complicated situation? Where would I even begin? And what if she did the role-playing thing? But I forced myself to meet her at least once.

Dr. Elliott, who I guessed was a little older than my forty years, was a pretty, petite woman who listened attentively as I tried to paint a picture of my life. Midway through my long, tearful, and disjointed monologue, I stopped and said, "Am I making any sense?"

"You are making perfect sense," she said, and so the healing began.

In my circle of friends who have children with disabilities, we have a phrase we use to describe whether or not a teacher, doctor, or friend understood our situation.

"Does she get it?"

"I don't think he gets it."

"I asked her if she got it, and she said, 'Do I get what?' She doesn't get it!"

A session with Rebecca was not the classic "And how did that make you feel?" kind of scenario. Rebecca was all about action. She saw the big picture and extracted truths and feelings like a skilled surgeon. What can we do to make your life more manageable? You need services. Here is how you get them. Need a new psychiatrist for Matthew? Rebecca knew the best. Your knee requires surgery? Call this guy and mention my name. You'll need help at home while you're healing, call this agency.

"You need to get help from the Regional Center of the Department of Developmental Services," she said, and I nodded reluctantly.

"I've been putting that off," I confessed. "Just the act of calling them is an admission that Matthew's condition is lifelong."

Rebecca told me not to weigh myself down by mourning about the future. She pointed out that our family was eligible for services now, such as trained caretakers. I could finally come up for air.

"The Regional Center will pay for several hours a month of help for Matthew. You could use the funds to hire a mentor for him and perhaps a babysitter for all three boys so that you and Peter can get a break."

With Rebecca's guidance, I made my way out of the loud restaurant with flying utensils that my life had become to a place where I could stand back and view my possibilities with long-lost optimism. Insomnia and anxiety had paralyzed me, and Rebecca explained, without talking down, that serotonin levels in the brain were changed by chronic stress; that medication with therapy was needed to get me back on track. She referred me to a psychiatrist, who prescribed an antidepressant, and she made sure that he and my regular doctor worked together on my behalf.

One day I got a call from an associate of Rebecca's. I had an appointment with Rebecca that day, but it turned out that she was very ill and would have to take some time off. I tried my best to find out the nature of the illness, but her colleague wouldn't tell me. I wanted to tell her that Rebecca and I were good friends, which I believed to be true, and that she would want me to know, but having heard in movies about "transference," when a patient mistakes therapy for friendship, I backed off.

I called a friend who also saw Rebecca, and we tried to figure out a way to find out more. I decided to call a few Bay Area hospitals to ask if she was a patient.

"Brilliant!" my friend said.

————

"Alta Bates Hospital," the operator answered.

"Yes, I'd like to deliver some flowers to Rebecca Elliott. What floor is she on?"

"She's on three." Bingo! "Would you like me to put you through?"

All of a sudden I felt like a stalker.

"No, no, I'll just swing by later with the flowers. Thank you!"

That afternoon, I tiptoed off the elevator on the third floor of Alta Bates Hospital with a small bouquet of flowers in a vase and went to the closest nurses' station.

"Will you see that Rebecca Elliott gets these?" I said to a young nurse at the desk, my feet poised in getaway stance.

"Oh, go right in!'" she said, gesturing toward room 3112, two feet away. "She's awake."

Feeling incredibly nervy and wildly over the line, I placed the flowers in front of room 3112. Didn't this woman know that Rebecca had to be protected from nuts like me?

"Oh, no. I don't want to bother her. She's my psychologist," I blurted as the nurse picked up the flowers and paused by the room, looking apprehensive.

So much for being discreet. I took off down the hall to the elevator, and once I got in, I laughed, thinking of what was transpiring in room 3112. I could see the smile on Rebecca's face as she saw who the flowers were from, and I knew we would share a laugh about this scene later. My father always says, "Never squelch a generous impulse." No matter what.

Thankfully, Rebecca recovered from her illness, and we did laugh about my brazen act of kindness. We talked briefly about her illness. But there was work to do, and Rebecca swiftly moved back to the business of bracing me for unknown challenges ahead.

CHAPTER 20

MOM IS SICK

IT WAS MOVING DAY, December 19, 1996. I was feeling great. I had been seeing Dr. Elliott weekly for a year, and while life was still complicated, I could handle it with calm, thanks not only to Rebecca's support, but to the antidepressant that was quieting my anxiety. Peter and I had been looking for a new house for six months, since the day when Matthew wandered onto a freeway on-ramp a few blocks near our first home. We had thought he was in his room at the time.

"Hi, Laura, this is Mary down the street. I'm sure you've been looking for Matthew. You won't believe where I found him."

But there was also good news about Matthew, now ten years old. Rebecca had encouraged Peter and me to have him evaluated by at psychiatrist at University of California in San Francisco, a premier center for the diagnosis and treatment of autism.

"I'm surprised that no one has suggested you see them before," she had said, and so was I. But the psychiatrist at UCSF recommended Ritalin to help Matthew stay focused in school, and Luvox to help curb his obsessive-compulsive behavior. After taking the Luvox for two weeks, Matthew's airport obsession evaporated, and his teacher noticed that he was more tuned in immediately after starting the Ritalin. Thankfully, Matthew appeared to tolerate both medications well.

There were many things that we loved about our new house. It was in the same town as our first house, but it was closer to schools and had a huge backyard. But the best thing about it was that Andy, who had always shared a room with Matthew, would now have a room of his own.

"We'll bring lunch on moving day!" my mother had said. My dad had recently retired and moved with my mom to Carmel, two hours away. Mom and I had been mentally preparing for their move for a long time and trying to convince each other that it would be better for everyone.

"Maybe we're too close," she said. "Maybe it's not healthy."

"You've worked hard to keep me going through it all," I replied. "It will be good for me to do more on my own. And I'm sure you could use a break."

"Let's face it," my mom concluded, choking up. "It's going to be awfully lonely, but we'll make it. We'll visit a lot and so will you."

In my heart, I knew that the move would be a healthy one for my mother. It was emotionally draining for her to watch me struggle with Matthew as he moved toward adolescence.

"I sure wish I could still help you with him," she said. "I love him so much, but he's just too much for me these days."

My dad and I had been worrying a lot about Mom's health lately. She became easily tired and short of breath. Her doctor explained that her lungs lacked elasticity due to scarring from childhood illnesses, and her asthma made matters worse. But when she was near the ocean, my dad noticed, she felt better.

Rain started to fall the minute the movers pulled away from our new house.

"That's what I call good luck," I said, smiling. "What time is it?"

"I don't believe it! It's already 3:30!" said Peter. "I'm starving."

"Where are Mom and Dad? They were going to bring lunch."

My parents were never late. They were always early. And on a day like today?

"Maybe they called and we didn't hear," said Peter. "Maybe they meant dinner. Where is that box of crackers?"

"We don't even have the phone plugged in!" I said, rifling through some boxes in the garage. I pulled one out and plugged it in.

You have two new messages.

First message sent Saturday at 10:45 a.m.

"Hi, Laura, it's Scott. Have you heard from Mom and Dad today? They were going to stop by on their way to your house. Just give me a call."

Second message sent Saturday at 12:49 p.m.

"Hi, sweetheart. Mom was having a little trouble breathing, so we took her to the emergency room just to check things out. Don't worry; she's where she needs to be. They're going to keep her overnight just to be safe. I'll call you later or you can try me. Love you."

What's the number, WHAT'S THE NUMBER!?

I called my brother—no answer. I slammed down the phone and then dialed 411.

"In Monterey, the number of Community Hospital."

"Mom, we're out of crackers," whined Matthew. "When will Grandma and Grandpa be here?"

"BE QUIET. I'M TRYING TO CALL THEM!" I yelled, slamming down the phone. All three boys started crying at once. Then the phone rang.

"Hi, Laura, it's Dad."

"What happened? Is she OK?"

"She's fine now that we're here. She was just having a tough time breathing and was really pale, so I brought her in. They're still checking her out and giving her an extra shot of oxygen. Hold on a moment, she wants to talk to you for just a minute."

"I'm fine," said my mom in slow motion, faint and muffled. "I sound goofy, but I'm fine."

"I love you, Mom!" I said.

"Laura," Dad said, taking the phone, "don't come down. Mom is already really anxious and she'll worry about your kids. Believe me, she's going to be fine."

"Dad, don't worry about me," I said. "Just call me when you know more."

"OK, sweetheart. How's the house?"

"Perfect. I love you."

CHAPTER 21

PEOPLE WHO CAME AROUND

I WORRIED ABOUT HOW MATTHEW WOULD FIT into the new neighborhood. I thought about circulating a flier that would explain him and his behavior, but I was so preoccupied with my mother's health that I never got around to it.

My father would later admit that he'd thought she would die the day he'd taken her to the emergency room from what turned out to be a blood clot in her lung and pulmonary fibrosis.

"But with the right medicine, respiratory therapy, and rest," said my ever-reassuring father, "she'll be on her feet in no time."

Our move to the new neighborhood coincided with Matthew's latest obsession, one that made us question the efficacy of Luvox, the drug meant to curb his obsessive-compulsive symptoms—balloons. I was guilty of launching the balloon phase when I started buying them for him as a reward for a good day at school. Then one day, Matthew saw an airplane fly overhead with a banner attached to it, and he started taping signs to his balloons. He would let the balloon go and imagine where it might land.

"This is a GRANDMA'S ALL BETTER NOW balloon," he said

once. "It's going all the way to Carmel."

I became keenly aware of how many damn balloons were *everywhere*. If I saw a balloon around town, I would make a mental note and take a different route when driving with Matthew.

Why? Because I knew that Matthew would not rest until any balloon in his path was freed. One time, he impulsively cut a balloon loose near a freeway, and it dipped down close to the speeding cars. I held my breath, shuddering to think of the disaster he could have caused.

One sunny Saturday, I was about to make the rounds of the neighborhood to search for Matthew, who had disappeared, when the doorbell rang.

Uh-oh.

I opened the door gingerly and saw my neighbor Sarah, hands on her hips, looking very angry. Sarah was a stunning blond in her mid-thirties with a handsome husband and two small sons. I had met her briefly when we had moved to the neighborhood a few months before, but we never connected. I had attributed this to our age difference—and to Matthew.

"I think your *son* stole a *balloon* off our *mail*box," she growled.

"Yes, I'm sure he did," I said. "I'll go get another one right now."

My keys and purse in the front hallway, I started toward the garage.

Sarah looked surprised by my cooperation, but a little frustrated that she couldn't finish her diatribe. I paused and let her finish.

"I have heard he steals a lot of balloons and—"

She stopped, seeing the anguish on my face.

"I know," I said, my voice cracking. Don't start crying, Laura. Just keep it together. "I'll be right back with the balloon."

And off I went, to the party store where they knew me well, feeling stupid. As I drove off, I saw Sarah stomp back to her house where a few couples were standing. I imagined their conversation.

"You went to old lady Shumaker's house? Wow! What's she like? Did you tell her off? Good! Where's she going now?"

I pulled up to Sarah's house eight minutes later with a red balloon and rang the doorbell. No answer. I heard the sounds of a birthday party behind the gate to their backyard and slipped through it. As I passed the garbage cans, garden tools, and blue plastic wading pool, about sixty multicolored balloons came into view. There were also streamers and HAPPY BIRTHDAY signs and a large piñata, but the sight of the balloons—she could have replaced the stolen balloon with one of them—floored me.

Sarah strode over, unfazed.

"Thank you," she said curtly, snatching the balloon.

I got the hell out of there.

After this incident, I tightened the reins on Matthew and avoided driving by Sarah's. "Tightening the reins" meant constant surveillance, which was not appreciated by my son. If I was distracted by a phone call or even a sneeze, Matthew would make a run for it. I tried to put myself in the position of Sarah and the other neighbors and could imagine them discussing us.

"I know the kid's got a problem, but they ought to. . . "

Ought to what? I had investigated tracking devices, but at that time they were only available for military and law enforcement. I thought a gadget that would deliver a beeping sound or a mild shock might work, but Dr. Hoffman advised against it. I had friends who monitored their kids with walkie-talkies, but they only work when both parties *agree* to stay in touch.

About a year after the Sarah incident, I got a call from another neighbor, Jean, a good friend of Sarah's, inviting me over. Was this an intervention? I thought. No, she and Sarah were having a neighborhood coffee and could I join the group? I said yes right away, thanked her, hung up the phone, and burst into tears.

Matthew was not my only worry at the time. My mother's health continued to deteriorate, and she now relied on oxygen apparatus to keep her going. I also worried about Andy, who had always been outgoing, but who had withdrawn considerably in the last year. He continued to do well in school and was well-liked, but he'd stopped having friends over and refused invitations. He had grown weary of the daily grind—the explanations, the outbursts, the lonely times when we were so preoccupied with managing Matthew. He didn't want to bother us with the ups and downs of *his* life. Peter and I asked Andy if he wanted to talk to a counselor about his feelings, and he said he did not. Looking back, I think he wanted to be removed from the category of those who needed therapeutic intervention, like Matthew.

While I needed my mother more than ever, I tried to protect her from my escalating difficulties with Matthew and saved them instead for my sessions with Rebecca. I thought I was a convincing actress, but Mom picked up the strain in my voice in our daily 8:00 a.m. call the morning of the neighborly gathering.

"Oh! And I'm getting together with some women in the neighborhood!"

"You mean the ones that don't like Matthew? No wonder you sound tense."

She went on to tell me that *obviously* these women could see what a wonderful person I was and were coming around.

"They need you more than you need them!"

She encouraged me to take a breath, have fun, and not to apologize too much for Matthew, her sweet grandson.

The morning of the gathering, I told Peter that I thought I'd skip it and go to the gym. As he left for work he hugged me and told me to go and have fun, and that I would be the best-looking woman there. In the end, I decided I would go and show these people that I *was* a wonderful person, once voted most friendly in my high-school senior class, and that I was doing my best in an arduous situation. But I was in the mood to blend in with the crowd, not to be seen as the mother of the strange kid.

I laughed to myself as I approached Jean's house with flowers from my garden in hand. Laura, your days of blending in are *over*. I marched forward, bolstered by the memory of my mother's encouraging words and Peter's loving smile as he had left for work that morning, knowing my trepidation.

I had visualized the gathering, walking in: a conference table in the living room, being encircled by the women of the neighborhood, fielding accusations as in a Senate hearing. Instead, I was absorbed into a group of friendly, good-looking women who ambled around a granite island in the kitchen, eating muffins, drinking coffee, and laughing a lot.

We talked about paint colors and kitchen remodels, babysitters and vacation spots. I tried to groove with the scene, but I had an overwhelming urge to clear the air by making a public apology about Matthew's disruptive behavior, and to take the question-and-answer session about which I had fantasized. Then I remembered my mother's advice and held back. The morning wasn't just about me.

After about an hour the group started to break up, and I started to head for home. I thanked Sarah and Jean, and as I left, Sarah called out to me.

"How is Matthew doing?" she asked.

Don't cry, Laura.

"A work in progress!" I joked. "I hope you'll let me know if he bothers you, I'm always available—"

Oh, no. She's coming toward me and being nice. "It must be so hard. Can I ask you a question?"

We sat on Jean's front porch, and Sarah asked me: When did you learn he was autistic? How do his brothers handle it? I noticed he likes to mow lawns—maybe he can mow mine some-time. We talked for an hour. I teared up, but I didn't cry. A few other women stopped by on their way out and joined in—they all made me feel like a hero, not like the crazy Shumaker lady with the weird kid.

Once home, I collapsed on the couch, relieved and wrung out. It had been a healing morning. I was grateful for the way it turned out, even more grateful that it was over. It occurred to me that my neighbors were hungry for information, and that my appearance this morning was a bridge-builder. They had a clearer picture of me, and of Matthew. I was approachable now, and so were they.

The next day, I called Jean to thank her.

"You are so welcome. I was actually just about to call you. Matthew is standing in front of my house, and a police car just pulled up to talk to him. You might want to run down and see what's going on."

I ran down as fast as I could. Matthew and the officer were all smiles.

"Hi. I'm his mother," I said breathlessly.

"Hello, I'm Officer Jones. Everything is fine. Matthew was just asking me if I take care of bad guys," he said, winking.

He got it.

"Goodbye, Officer Jones," said Matthew, grinning.

"Remember what I told you, Matthew," said the officer, pulling away, "No more throwing rocks at cars, especially police cars!"

I was relieved that the police officer had been kind, but frustrated that Matthew's negative method of making a connection had succeeded. Would he throw a rock again in an attempt to make a friend? I looked over and saw Jean standing on her porch.

"You OK?" she asked, and I just rolled my eyes. "Hang in there," she said, her front door shutting behind her.

CHAPTER 22

ADOLESCENCE

ONE EARLY SUMMER MORNING a few months after the healing neighborhood gathering, I went for a walk with my friend Diane, whose fifteen-year-old son is also autistic. Diane and I found great comfort in sharing each other's trials, and while our sons had very different interests and quirks, we were able to help each other—brainstorming, venting, and laughing through tears.

I filled her in on how Matthew was doing, and on my mom's health, which remained fragile. I missed her daily presence in my life.

"Peter worked at home a lot this summer so that I could spend time with her," I said.

It was hard being away from Peter and the boys so much, but to my surprise they thrived, developing a pattern that worked so well, I felt left out when I was home. I was grateful, though, to see Peter and Matthew's relationship blossom. Peter had naturally gravitated toward Andy and John for fun and companionship in the years since Matthew's diagnosis, and he was surprised by how well he connected with Matthew in my absence.

"So Matthew's in a great spot for now," I told Diane.

"That's good," said Diane, "because he's probably heading into puberty, and let me tell you, it's not pretty."

"Matthew is just twelve now," I said, "and still a little boy. I think he's going to be a later bloomer."

"Maybe," chuckled Diane, "but brace yourself!"

I just didn't want to hear it, Diane could tell, and she backed off. "Things with Matthew are going well now, and I just want to enjoy it. Besides," I said, "I heard that sometimes people with autism actually calm down during adolescence."

"Uh-huh," Diane said, smiling. "That'd be nice."

The following Sunday, our family went to church. There were times when my three boys were all lined up and we seemed like a typical nice-looking family. John, at five, had white-blond hair and rosy cheeks, and his large hazel eyes were set far apart, which made him look perpetually innocent. Ten-year-old Andy, who had always appeared confident beyond his years, was solid and compact, his shining eyes matching his light-brown hair. And then there was Matthew, who at twelve was the most handsome of the group. He had Peter's rosy complexion, a heart-shaped face, and golden blond hair. His mouth was fixed in a dreamy smile, as if he were withholding a private joke. Just when people were about to say, "Autistic? You would never know," Matthew's face would suddenly break into a large grimace-like smile. His whole body looked so full of fuel that he needed to jump, and jump he did, waving his hands and dipping to touch the ground as a tiny bit of drool spilled over his lip.

Matthew usually went to Sunday school with a teen volunteer who helped keep him under control, but today was Family

Worship Sunday, when the children remained with the adults throughout the service.

Our family usually stayed home from church on Family Worship Sunday because it was a challenge for Matthew to sit still for a full hour. He'd stretch his arms over his head and lean back lazily. A pencil and a pad of paper was always on hand to occupy him when he got squirmy, but he often got so excited by what he was drawing that he would squeal and laugh. Our congregation had known Matthew since his toddlerhood, and people were tolerant of him, but I couldn't blame them for snickering and scowling from time to time when his outbursts disrupted their concentration.

The five of us took our seats, and I studied the order of worship.

"Oh good," I told Peter, "it's communion Sunday. We can sneak out after communion if Matthew gets restless."

In our Presbyterian church, communion is served while parishioners sit in the pews. Deacons circulate large silver trays of bread and thimble-sized glasses of grape juice.

But when it came time for communion, the deacons didn't march to the front of the church with the trays.

"Today," said our pastor, "we are going to try something new. We will celebrate communion through the practice of intinction. We'd like to invite you to come forward and partake of the bread and wine and then return to your seat."

Peter rolled his eyes. "Maybe you should just sit here with Matthew," he whispered.

"NO," Matthew yelled. "I want to be like everyone else! I want to get the bread and juice!"

"Shhhh," I whispered. "That's fine. Just be a good boy."

"I *will!*" he yelled back, drawing stares.

We were sitting at the back of the church, so we had to wait awhile for our turn.

A deep, throaty, unfamiliar laugh erupted from Matthew, and when I shushed him again, I noticed it: At first I thought he must have stuck the pencil he'd been drawing with in his pants to cause the fabric to strain so dangerously.

"Matthew, take the pencil out of your pants," I whispered.

Matthew's brown eyes found mine.

"It's not a pencil," he replied, grinning broadly.

Peter, unaware of the situation, was already heading down the aisle with Andy and John.

"Matthew," I whispered desperately. "We have to stay here," but it was too late. He stood up—I couldn't believe my eyes— and started to walk down the aisle.

"Matthew, you need to stand *right* next to me." I looked down as we walked. Now what had first looked like a pencil more closely resembled a flagpole.

God? Please help me. Please let Matthew be invisible just for a few minutes.

The best I could do was walk forward, avoiding all eye contact, with a straight face. When Matthew and I got to the altar, I glanced at him again. It was still there. He still had that goofy grin.

Matthew darted ahead of me and took a piece of bread, dipped it into the grape juice, and snickered his way back to the pew. I could just hear Peter saying later "Oh, I'm sure no one noticed," and I would tell him "Oh yes they did, and what the hell."

"Shall we sneak out?" I asked Peter once we were all seated after communion.

"Matthew seems to be doing fine" was his answer, and I thought about what Diane had said earlier that week.

I realized my life was entering a new phase.

CHAPTER 23

LIGHTENING UP

MATTHEW'S "ONSLAUGHT OF PUBERTY" PHASE was well under-way by the time he was thirteen and beginning his eighth-grade year, and it coincided with another less threatening phase. Matthew started making signs.

When it was my turn to host the Book Club meeting, he would tape a "WELCOME BOOK CLUB" sign to the mantle of the fireplace, and my friends smiled politely. When we ordered pizza, the delivery boy would find a sign on the door that read "LARGE CHEESE PIZZA WELCOME." The signs embarrassed eleven-year-old Andy, but he knew that if he tried to disrupt Matthew's rituals, an explosive scene would ensue.

During this same period, I hired a college student, Chad, to hang out with Matthew after school. Chad was a good-looking ex-Marine with a big heart who liked to look in the mirror a lot. When he picked Matthew up at school, the eighth-grade girls would swoon.

"He is, like, *totally* good-looking!" I heard one of them say as the two sauntered off.

I had instructed Chad to take Matthew out into the community, help him learn safety rules, conduct appropriate interactions with store clerks, and work on table manners at the pizza parlor. I'm sure the program didn't always go as I envisioned, but at least I got a break.

I knew Matthew was connecting with Chad when signs started showing up. "GO AWAY CHAD." "CHAD YOU'RE A GIRL." Matthew was exhilarated, downright joyful, about Chad's reaction to his signs, ripping them down dramatically and then running after Matthew with a squirt gun.

Matthew's primary method of connecting with people continued to be this kind of teasing, and I told Chad it might not be good to allow it to continue.

"Lighten up," Chad laughed in return. "We're having fun, that's all."

One day, while I was getting the kids ready for school, Peter and I had some sort of argument. I don't remember what it was about, but it was one of those arguments not settled before he left for work, leaving feelings of anger to fester all day. By noon I was in such a state that I felt the need to call him, tell him off, and then hang up the phone before he could respond. What made me crazier was that he didn't call right back to set things straight. I learned later that the poor guy had been in a tense meeting and couldn't.

By three o'clock, I was psychotic. I had just picked Matthew up from school and learned from his teacher that he had had a bad day. Some students had dared him to go into the girls' bathroom, prompting the girls to yell "*Pervert!*"

Matthew had a mischievous smile on his face as he asked me

if Chad was coming over today. Yes, he was. Thank God.

While I waited for Chad to arrive, my friend Susie dropped by. She had called earlier, noticed I was on the edge, and wanted to check on me. Before I could tell her my story, the doorbell rang. Probably Chad, I thought, relieved. It wasn't Chad, but the local florist with a beautiful arrangement of flowers with a sealed note and a nervous, almost frightened look on her face.

"Thanks. I *deserve* these!" I yelled hoarsely.

She handed me the flowers from Peter and took off before I could give her a tip. The poor thing. I must have looked as deranged as I felt. I'll stop by the shop tomorrow and thank her, I thought, and explain my situation.

Chad showed up a few minutes later, and Matthew ran out to greet him before he could get to the door. I followed with money for pizza, and off they went. As I walked back to the front door, I saw it: a new sign taped on the front door. In dark, angry scrawl, it read "i hate you chad." The mystery of the terrified florist was solved. She must have concluded the flowers from Peter were from a beleaguered husband named Chad.

Susie and I laughed hard and long. We kept trying to pull ourselves together, only to convulse in laughter again, thinking of the terrorized florist. This blessed release of tension didn't just result from the resolution of the morning's argument. It resulted from all the phases and stages I had been through and all those looming in the future. Always trying to appear the upbeat, in-control mother of this strange child had taken its toll on me.

Just then Matthew burst through the front door with an impish smile and pizza sauce on his face and in his hair, Chad close behind.

"Hi, guys! How'd it go?"

"Well, it wasn't Matthew's day."

CHAPTER 24

JOHN

I WAS STILL LAUGHING on and off about the I HATE YOU CHAD incident, but the Monday-afternoon phone message from Mr. Turner, John's second-grade teacher, brought me back to earth.

"John's had kind of a tough day," it said. "Some kids were teasing him about Matthew. Thought you might like to know."

Damn it, I knew this would happen.

The Saturday before, John had a soccer game. Peter was out of town, and the helper I had scheduled to watch Matthew was sick, so I had no choice but to take Matthew with us to the game.

"John, Chad can't watch Matthew today. Do you mind if he comes to watch your game?"

"No, I don't mind. Are you snack lady? Will you bring dough-nuts?"

When I looked at John, I still saw a wide-eyed baby with the sunny personality that matched the golden peach fuzz on his head. At seven, he was still a cheerful blond with a generous spirit, and he was growing into the biggest and sturdiest of my three boys.

Like many third children, John spent a lot of time observing the world from his car seat in the minivan, riding with his brothers to and from school, soccer, and doctors' appointments. Before he learned to walk, he laughed from his bouncy seat as he watched his brothers run through the sprinklers, ride bikes, and build tall towers with blocks, only to knock them down. Matthew and Andy's favorite activity was putting John in the bed of a large Tonka truck and launching him down the carpeted hall. John smiled and laughed through it all while I prepared nervously, but happily, to avert crash landings.

When John was five, he asked why Matthew went to a different school on a yellow school bus, and why he jumped and flapped his hands and laughed at strange things. By the age of six, he felt badly for Matthew because he didn't have any friends. Lately John had been bothered by Matthew's impulsive actions—throwing toys over the fence, running from one room to another just to strike him or Andy, disrupting happy family time by turning over a game board or dropping the dice down the heater vent.

During John's soccer game, Matthew sat quietly at first on the grass near the goal post, but then the sound of an airplane brought him to his feet, and he jumped and flapped his hands, as a bead of spittle ran down the corner of his mouth. I saw a few of the soccer players on the sidelines exchanging glances and snickering. I searched for John, who was playing goalie.

Good, he's oblivious.

Then one of the boys started to imitate Matthew, generating gales of laughter from his buddies, until his mother saw what was going on and sternly grabbed her son by the arm. Thank you, I

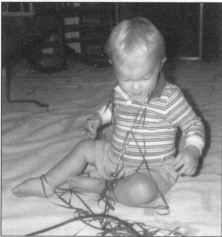

ABOVE: Peter and Laura Shumaker with their firstborn, Matthew, in San Francisco, May 22, 1986: "We were both so excited to become parents."

LEFT: At six months, Matthew was already drawn to strange play objects, content in his own world.

FACING PAGE: A dreamy and remote Matthew at three.

THIS PAGE, LEFT: Baby Andy joined big brother Matthew, before the diagnosis of autism.

BELOW: Three-year-old Matthew, exploring the garden.

BOTTOM: Matthew, 4, and Andy, 2, at their grandparents' house in Piedmont, California.

LEFT: Matthew, 6, soon after his autism diagnosis. Balloons had become one of his obsessions.

BELOW: A day in the park with brothers John, 4; Matthew, 10; and Andy, 8. Matthew's mischievous moods were getting on Andy's nerves; John was still happily oblivious.

FACING PAGE: Matthew's obsession with machines and orderly straight lines found a practical application in the careful mowing and trimming of lawns. The lawn mower was a gift from his grandpa.

LEFT: A somber Matthew and classmates, during his first and only year at the local high school.

BELOW LEFT: Matthew with his grandpa on Graduation Day at Beaver Run, June 2004.

BELOW RIGHT: Laura and her beloved mother, Susie.

BOTTOM: John, 13; Andy, 18; and Matthew, 20; with their Uncle Scott's children Melissa, 23; Greg, 20; and Kelly, 18.

LEFT: Matthew as Dr. Faust in Camphill's graduation play.

BELOW: Camphill teacher Guy Alma, the play's director, rehearsing a student.

BOTTOM: Matthew with Camphill mentor David Schwartz.

ABOVE: The best-trimmed lawn in Lafayette, California is the backdrop for this protrait of Laura with Matthew, John, and Andy.

told her, my heart beating, my eyes darting back and forth between John and Matthew. Both seemed unaware of the taunting.

Then it was halftime.

The seven-year-old players bunched together for orange slices and a pep talk from the coach. I noticed a few of the boys saying something to John, who said something in response at which the boys burst into laughter. John smiled, the whistle blew, and the game continued. Matthew spent the rest of the game swinging high on a swing nearby. I could relax.

When the game was over, I couldn't throw doughnuts and juice boxes to the boys fast enough.

"John! Matthew! Time to go!"

I was heaving the picked-over doughnuts into the trashcan when the Team Mom thanked me for bringing snacks.

"Will you offer something a little more healthy next time?"

It's not my style to tell people where to shove their granola bars, so I just said "Sure" and left.

John seemed fine as we were driving back. I waited until we got home to ask him privately what he and the boys were laughing about at halftime.

"They said Matthew was crazy, and I said, 'Well, you know what they say about teenagers.' But Mom, can I invite a friend over?"

Mr. Turner had left the message at lunchtime. It was now 1:30. I pulled into the parking lot of John's school at 1:42 and dashed to room 4, peeking into the classroom. When John saw me, he flew from his seat and into my arms.

Mr. Turner motioned to me that he would call me later, as John ran to me, his lower lip trembling and his chest heaving. I thought I would have the right words when this time came but I was at a loss. His sobbing finally ended with a heavy sigh, and I asked him what had happened.

"They were jumping up and down and shaking their hands all around at recess and they were laughing. What does 'retard' mean?" John asked, his eyes searching for the sanctuary of our gray minivan.

"It's a mean way of saying someone is—different, that their brain works differently," I answered.

Those little sons of bitches.

"They said *Matthew* was a retard," John cried incredulously.

"Awww, let's go home. Andy will be home soon and we can all go out for ice cream."

"What about Matthew?"

"Chad is picking him up from school today. They're going to play basketball."

"Maybe we can bring some ice cream home for him," he said, wiping his eyes on my sleeve. "Why are you crying, Mom?"

"Because you are so nice."

Sometimes the best view is from the rearview mirror of a minivan. On the way to the ice cream parlor, Andy and John shared Matthew stories and strategies, with our black lab Katie sitting sympathetically between them, her eyebrows alternating up and down as they talked and laughed. Not all of their conversation focused on what to do when people said things about Matthew. There was a lot of healthy venting, and I let the comments fly. But soon enough, they were back to sharing Matthew stories affectionately.

"Remember the time he asked the dwarf if he was a boy or a man?"

"Yeah! That guy got really mad!"

"How about the time Mom's friend came over, and Matthew asked her when she was going to leave?"

"Wait, wait! What about the time he asked Mr. Harris how old he was, and when he said he was eighty-six, Matthew said, 'So you'll be dying soon.'"

John and Andy shook the car with their laughter, and Katie seemed to be smiling along with their joy. Why couldn't I laugh with them?

"The poor kid," said Andy, wiping the tears of laughter on his sweatshirt. At twelve, he sounded like a sage old man who had already traveled down a difficult path.

"Yeah. Poor Matthew," John said, as we pulled up to the ice cream parlor. He raced in to survey the tubs of ice cream behind the glass.

"Look," he said, "they have Matthew's favorite, bubblegum ice cream! Can we get some for him, Mom?"

The view from my rearview mirror changed on the way home. The afternoon sun fell gently on Andy's light-brown hair as he looked quietly out the window, and John cradled our dog Katie's head in his lap, stroking it tenderly. A bond had been strengthened in the wake of heartbreak and hurt feelings. Brothers came together in laughter and in sorrow, and they were left feeling the weight of their family's bittersweet burden. But would they hold each other up in the years before them? Would they have the strength to hold Matthew up and guide him when we were gone?

The bubblegum ice cream had melted slightly by the time we rolled into the driveway at home. As Chad and Matthew pulled up beside us, I got the feeling that something was up.

"We got you bubblegum ice cream, Matthew!" said John, holding out the dripping mess proudly.

"I'll eat it later, *OK*?" Matthew shot back. "I'm in a bad mood!" He stomped into the house and slammed the door.

John, Andy, and I paused for a moment and then burst out laughing.

"Well John, you tried," Andy laughed.

The boys followed Matthew into the house, and I stood outside for a moment and took a breath.

Don't worry, John. Matthew will remember.

CHAPTER 25

THE SURPRISE

IT WAS A BEAUTIFUL APRIL AFTERNOON in Lafayette. John, who had recovered cheerfully from the teasing incident at school, was building a fort and trying to coax the dog inside with a milk bone. Matthew, approaching his fourteenth birthday, was sitting at the kitchen table painting with watercolors, the sun catching his blond hair through the window, and Andy had just rushed out to baseball practice, trailing sunflower seeds from the torn pocket of his grass-stained baseball pants. We had had our share of bumpy days lately, but this was not one of them. I walked through our front door to clip some roses when I noticed the mail had just come.

In the midst of catalogs and bills was an official-looking envelope addressed to Mr. and Mrs. Peter Shumaker. It got my attention.

On letterhead from the offices of attorney Casper White, it read:

"I am writing you regarding the bicycle accident involving your son, Matthew, on March 8, 2002 [about a month before] blah, blah, blah, I am representing so-and-so who was injured in the accident, please contact me, etc."

I walked into the kitchen where Matthew was painting and asked, "Did you have an accident on your bike?"

"Who told you?" Mathew replied calmly.

"Someone wrote me a letter about it. Were you hurt?"

"Not really."

"Who else was in the accident?"

"A boy."

Oh, my God.

"Was he hurt?"

"Probably."

"Was he bleeding?"

"Pretty much."

God help me.

"Matthew," my voice quaking, "did an ambulance come?"

"I give up. I'm done talking about this."

He resumed painting, at which point I lost it.

"Matthew! I need to know what happened! Where did this happen? Was there anyone there that you know? Did anyone ask you questions?"

Matthew's lower lip quivered as he tapped his paintbrush nervously on the table. "Am I in trouble?" he whimpered.

I took a breath and said, "No, of course not. You just paint and we'll talk about this later."

I hugged him and he choked back a few sobs. After I got him to relax, he started painting again and I went back to my bedroom and called the attorney, my eye on the blue bike in the backyard.

Mr. White, the attorney, explained to me that his client and his nine-year-old son, who had just moved to our community from Poland in the last few months, were riding bikes at the middle school around the corner from our house. He said that Matthew and his client's son had collided. Matthew had stopped for a moment, then fled. The nine-year-old had broken his leg. Badly. Had to be in a wheelchair for six weeks. The family had no medical insurance.

"I understand your son is autistic."

My mind raced to the conclusions made by the Polish family, the attorney, and the community. This thirteen-year-old autistic boy is riding his bike without supervision, collides with and injures a child, and leaves the scene. His parents are negligent. He is a danger to those around him.

"He wants to ride his bike at the playground like any thirteen-year-old. I can't watch him every second," I countered.

But I knew that unlike other thirteen-year-old boys, he did not have the judgment needed to manage these kinds of situations. I had hired after-school helpers to take him for bike rides and other activities, but Matthew was not supervised every second. I tried to keep track of him, but he snuck out regularly.

People in my community often said to me, "I always see you driving around looking for something. Does your dog get out?" No, my son does.

The attorney informed me that our homeowners' insurance would take care of the medical costs and told me to have the company contact him. I couldn't wait to get off the phone to call an attorney friend of mine, but remembered to ask one last question. How did you get Matthew's name and address? Mr. White had gotten the information from a neighbor who didn't want to be identified.

It hurt me that a neighbor didn't call us first. I could have explained that Matthew probably fled the scene because he was scared, overwhelmed, and incapable of processing what had happened. Now all of this time had gone by, leaving the neighbor's accusations and assumptions to fester and spread throughout the community. If only I had kept better track of Matthew.

As I worried about the injured boy, damage control became a priority. I wanted to call the family and see how the boy was doing and perhaps bring him a toy and the parents a bottle of wine, but I knew I shouldn't. Maybe I could find the neighbor who had reported Matthew and assure him we would be more vigilant. A gift would help this witness spread the word that we were actually wonderful people. I thought about putting together a flier describing Matthew and his disability, maybe even sending one to the local newspaper. No. The flier might be misconstrued as a warning: "In case you see him tearing around on his bike, watch out!"

Peter and I kept our eyes open for a nine-year-old boy in a wheelchair, but we never saw him. We heard that he was expected to make a full recovery, and we were grateful. It could have been so much worse.

The incident forced us to consider the idea of finding a residential school for Matthew. At least find out what's out there, we told each other.

CHAPTER 26

MIDDLE SCHOOL IS HARD

I SAT IN THE PARKING LOT of the school where Andy was a sixth-grader and Matthew was an eighth-grader. We lived right around the corner, and neither boy needed a ride. But my eyes were fastened on the path that Matthew would cross on his way home. Since the bicycle incident, I shadowed Matthew secretly, always ready to intervene when needed.

A friend who had a son Andy's age pulled up into the space next to me, her Volvo station wagon stuffed with groceries.

"Oh, my gosh!" I said. "You must be having a party."

"I wish!" she sighed dramatically. "Davey and his friends go through this much every few days! I mean, I love having all of his friends over, but I'm thinking about charging admission!"

"I hear you!" I chuckled.

Rub it in.

Ours had never been the house where the friends came to hang out and eat food, and I was jealous. I also worried that Andy didn't accept invitations.

"The last time I went to a friend's house," Andy had said, "they asked me why we never hang out at *my* house. I don't want to say 'because my brother might do something idiotic.'"

I understood, but I missed seeing Andy's old friends so much that when I ran into them on the street, I came on way too strong, embarrassing myself and Andy.

Derek! It's so good to see you! Look how TALL you've gotten!

The bell rang, and Matthew came hopping out of his classroom. I slid down behind my steering wheel.

"BOO," Andy yelled, sneaking up behind me. "What are you doing, Mom?"

"Shhh!" I said, pointing at Matthew. Right at that moment a group of smiling boys approached Matthew. They didn't know I was watching. At first I thought "How great! These kids are reaching out to him." And then they were circling him, asking him questions, telling him to pull his pants down.

"MATTHEW!" screamed Andy. "Don't do that!"

Matthew smiled and looked our way, and Andy ducked into the backseat.

"Matthew! It's time to go," I called out. The boys peeled off, and Matthew skipped to the car happily.

"Matthew! Never let people tease you like that," Andy said, visibly shaken.

"They weren't teasing me, Andy. They're my friends," he boasted.

"Friends don't tell you to pull your pants down!" I yelled. Matthew started to cry, heartbroken and embarrassed.

"Mom?" he sobbed, "what *do* friends do?" He cried on the short ride home, and Andy looked out the window, stunned.

"Let's play Nintendo," said Andy to Matthew once home,

and the two disappeared for about an hour.

"He's OK now," said Andy, emerging from Matthew's room. "Will you make me a milkshake?"

"Andy, I am so sorry," I said. "You must have been so embarrassed."

"If it's OK, I don't really want to talk about it."

Andy wandered outside and kicked his soccer ball around for a little while, then threw the tennis ball for the dog. He fiddled with his guitar; he did his homework. I stayed clear while staying close, and finally he spoke up.

"You know what I've been wondering?" he asked. "I've been wondering if I would be mean like that, if I didn't have a brother like Matthew."

"I don't think so," I said, hugging him.

"Yeah, I hope not," he replied.

Andy must have known that I would work on a way to reward him for his resilience, for his kindness. What he didn't know was that my judgment was clouded by my jealous encounter with the mother in the white Volvo.

"I'm going to give Andy a surprise party for his twelfth birthday," I announced to Peter that evening.

"He is not going to want that," warned Peter, "unless it's just a family party."

"No, I just think he needs a little help, a shove," I said. "I'll get Matthew out of here and invite some of his old friends. Andy's been wanting a ping-pong table. We can get him one and have it all set up when he gets home from school, and then when the friends surprise him, we can have a tournament with surprises and everything."

"Andy wants a ping-pong table?" Peter asked. "Are you sure you're not the one who wants him to have a ping-pong table?"

Andy came home from school the day of the party, dropped his backpack on the floor, and downed a glass of milk.

"Wow," he said, "the house is so clean."

"Why don't you go see how the backyard looks?" I asked, sweeping my hand like a hostess on a game show. The ping-pong table was draped with a tarp and wrapped with a goofy red bow.

"Is this my birthday present?" Andy asked, looking confused. "Shouldn't we wait until the family party?"

I already knew that I'd made a mistake. When "the guys" emerged from the garden shed and yelled *surprise*, Andy shot me a pained and desperate look, as if he knew he had let me down for not being one of them. He turned and put a smile on for the boys, but it was as if an army surrounded him, guns drawn.

At once it occurred to me that butterflies can't be forced from their cocoons—they need to emerge when the time is right. He put his best face on, but I could tell Andy was deeply hurt by my brazen disregard for his feelings. After the awkward party ended—and I moved it along as quickly as I could—I held Andy and apologized as he sobbed in my arms. As I held him, I could tell that he knew what I was trying to do, and that I meant well. But why would I want to change anything about this wonderful boy?

Finally, after Andy and I mopped up after the big surprise, he looked up at me, his face swollen from crying, his eyes shining with appreciation, and he thanked me for the ping-pong table. We laughed at my super-mom attempts, especially the addition of Joe Athlete and Charismatic Carl, whom Andy barely knew. Someday, I hoped, the pain of this day would evaporate and become a legendary chapter in our family's history.

But Andy's twelfth birthday was an important lesson to me. It became clear to me that Andy was *still* Andy, and as he struggled in silence to define himself, he was building strength, like the butterfly, preparing for a glorious flight from his cocoon.

CHAPTER 27

LOSING IT

JUST DAYS AFTER ANDY'S BIRTHDAY DEBACLE, I struck out again
with Matthew's fourteenth birthday party, inviting the students in
his special class for pizza, cake, and ice cream. Matthew had been
distancing himself from them lately in favor of the best-looking
and most popular "regular" kids at his school. I'd invited a few
of them, too, but they declined. On the Friday afternoon of
Matthew's party, he refused to come out of his room, yelling,
"I'm not special! Tell them to leave!"

The day after, I sat on the sofa that looks out our living room
window, my attention torn between the *People* magazine in my
lap and Matthew, who was sitting cross-legged on the front lawn,
inspecting—or was he dismembering?—a dead butterfly. A heap
of laundry on and around the coffee table nagged at me, but I
was just too tired, too scattered. Peter wandered in from the
kitchen, beer in hand.

"Where's Matthew?"

"Right there," I said frostily, motioning toward Matthew.

Saturdays were hard and seemed to go on forever. Someone
always had to keep track of Matthew, and one of us always

thought he or she was doing more than the other. I was discouraged that the bond that had strengthened between Peter and Matthew the previous summer had deteriorated, and Peter seemed to have given up on rebuilding it.

"What am I supposed to do?" Peter argued. "He never wants to do anything with me."

"You need to do the things that he likes to do," I suggested.

"Great, like wandering around the neighborhood and playing with balloons? He needs to learn to do the kinds of things kids his age do."

"Peter, kids his age hang out with their friends. That is not going to happen with Matthew without your help!"

I took a breath.

"Look, I do the best I can," I continued, "but Matthew doesn't want to be with his mother all the time. You need to think of something the two of you can do together."

Peter threw up his hands and left the room.

In earlier days, Peter took Matthew to Tilden Park for train and merry-go-round rides—over and over again. Later, they went for hikes, to the movies, and to a small local airport to watch the planes take off for hours. But at age fourteen, Matthew bolted from home whenever we blinked, craving the company of kids his age. He found it only with those who teased him, challenging him to spitting contests and daring him, unsuccessfully, to smoke pot.

"That stuff smells bad," Matthew said with disgust.

I was constantly searching for him, trying to redirect him and running out of steam, and I resented Peter for not doing more. To make matters worse, the erection that Matthew had first had in church a couple years back was there more often than not, drawing stares, laughter, and gossip. Mothers warned their daughters of all ages to steer clear of him. It made me feel terrible, but I didn't blame them.

Suddenly, the view out of our living room window changed, and I felt my feet planting firmly into the red Oriental carpet, ready to act. An elderly Asian woman and her husband walked by our house slowly and said something to Matthew. The woman was shaking her head and pointing at the butterfly that Matthew was "playing" with.

"Uh-oh," Peter and I mumbled in unison. Before we could move, Matthew picked up a rock and hurled it at the woman, hitting her in the shoulder.

Peter flew out the front door, grabbed Matthew, and dragged him inside while I apologized profusely to the couple. It was clear they didn't speak English, so I clarified Matthew's situation by pointing at him, then pointing my index finger at my temple, twirling it around and saying "Crazy."

They nodded sympathetically and went on their way.

By the time I got into the house, things were heating up.

"She didn't look nice!" Matthew yelled at Peter, who gripped Matthew's upper arm firmly.

Uh-oh. Peter's going to lose it.

"You don't throw *rocks* at people who *look* at you funny when you are doing something *FREAKY!*" Peter roared.

Matthew went nuts and started punching and scratching his father. It seemed that Matthew became stronger with every meltdown.

"Don't hit back!" I yelled at Peter, who succeeded in pinning Matthew to the hardwood floor.

I could tell Peter was tempted. This wasn't the first time Matthew had attacked. Peter and I have jagged scars on our hands and arms from similar incidents.

Matthew got loose and kicked a hole in the wall before I could pick up the phone and call 911.

Within a minute, the doorbell rang. I opened the door, and there stood Officer Jones, the policeman who had asked Matthew not to throw rocks at his police car, in his navy-blue uniform, complete with badge, gun in holster, and club.

I had never seen a tense situation defuse so magically.

The first person to speak was Matthew.

"Oops," he said, as if everything that had taken place had been accidental. A piece of sheetrock lay at his feet, its powder covering his right calf.

Officer Jones was of medium height and build, with a black crewcut and a passive expression on his face, like a young Joe Friday. He spoke calmly and quietly.

"Please tell me what happened," he said. There wasn't a hint of anger or threat in his voice.

"The lady didn't look nice," Matthew explained, "and I sort of threw a rock at her."

"And *I* told him you don't *attack* people who *look* at you funny!" Peter injected, heating up once again.

Officer Jones's expression remained spookily unchanged.

"Mrs. Shumaker called 911 because of a domestic altercation. Who started it?" he asked smoothly.

"*Autistic*," I whispered to the officer from over his right shoulder. He looked at me as if I were bonkers, but he paused and processed my clue while Matthew proceeded.

"I sort of hit my dad first, but then he hit me next."

God help us.

"Matthew, I didn't hit you," Peter said, glancing sideways at the policeman. "I held you down so you would stop hitting me and kicking holes in the wall!"

I looked at Peter and cringed. Normally a buttoned-up kind of guy, today he happened to be wearing a white threadbare undershirt with two small holes an inch above his left nipple. I scanned the room for his beer bottle and casually kicked some unfolded laundry behind the couch. A bra got tangled around my ankle, and I stumbled to regain my balance.

The officer seemed unmoved, and his ponderous silence made us nervous. After a moment, he spoke.

"Matthew, your father is right. You must never throw rocks at people. If someone upsets you, find a parent and let one of them handle things. You must never hit your parents. Do you understand?"

"Am I going to jail?" Matthew whimpered, obviously humiliated to have disappointed this powerful figure.

"No."

"Can I talk to you for a minute?" Matthew asked the officer, his voice quavering, his expression pained. I could tell he was hurt by the gulf that had formed between us. "I don't want my parents to hear."

Peter and I listened from the next room while Matthew and

the officer talked on the couch. I could see only the upper-right quadrant of the officer's face. Matthew told him how hard it was when people made fun of him. He told him how lonely he feels when his brothers go out with friends, and he has no one to hang out with.

"I have friends," he said, "but they're really busy."

Matthew told Officer Jones that girls look nice, and that he would like to be able to touch their hair, even though it's against the rules, and that his grandma was really sick and might die. The officer listened, the expression on his face softening ever so slightly. Just as Matthew was about to show him his room and his middle-school yearbook, the officer's radio stuttered—something about a shoplifting incident at the convenience store on the main drag.

"It was nice talking to you, Matthew. Will you remember what we talked about?"

"I surely will," Matthew said resolutely. "Do you think you can come over again if I need to talk?"

My poor lonely boy. He had made a connection, a friend. I never thought there would be a day when I would want a police call to last a little longer.

"Matthew, I am happy to talk with you, but I never want to come to this house again if you have thrown a rock, or hit your parents, or put a hole in the wall. Do you understand?"

"Do you ever shoot bad guys?" Matthew asked, trying to keep things going a little longer.

"Only if I have to. I really have to take this," he said as his radio crackled with urgency. "But you'll remember what we talked about?" he asked, placing his hand gently on Matthew's shoulder. Matthew nodded his assent, tears welling up in his eyes.

Matthew walked his new friend to his car. I thought I heard him ask the officer if he'd ever had a seizure. I stood with Matthew, patting his back lightly as he watched the police cruiser drive away.

"Does Officer Jones think I'm a good guy or a bad guy?" Matthew sputtered.

"He thinks you are a wonderful guy." I said.

"I'm not going to jail?" Matthew asked, his chest heaving.

"No, honey. You're not." And Matthew fell against me and cried tears of relief, regret, and confusion.

Matthew didn't notice the curious neighbors peering out their windows.

I'll give them a call later.

But what could I tell them to preserve Matthew's dignity?

"I hope he gets those bad guys," Matthew said, trying to pull himself together.

"I'm sure he will. Let's get you a cold washcloth and a drink of water."

"I'm a good guy," Matthew muttered, as we walked back into the house. I drenched a washcloth in ice-cold water and held it to his face as long as he would let me, and he went in his room and shut the door.

Peter and I sat at the dining room table, wiped out. We felt exposed, sad for Matthew, guilty for letting things fly out of control. We marveled at how quickly Matthew responded to the police officer, and we resolved to use his approach the next time.

But could we do it? Could we be firm and remain calm when Matthew threw a rock at someone, or kicked a hole in the wall, or reappeared after we had been searching for him for two hours? I could be a good actress, I thought. There was no way I could do it otherwise.

"I'm sorry," said Peter, looking down and shaking his head. "I'm so sorry."

"I know," I said. "I know it's hard, but we have to be patient."

"I just need to find a way to connect with him," he said, his voice cracking. "It's so *frustrating*."

"We'll figure something out," I said, squeezing his hand. Peter looked incredibly sad, and my heart ached for him. He got up from the table and went to see Matthew in his room. I heard them talking quietly, then laughing, and when they emerged, Matthew announced that they were going out for ice cream, "just me and Dad," and off they went.

I tried to think back on the last time my parents had "lost it" with me. It had been many, many years ago, and I didn't recall the details. But I did remember feeling alone and scared. I craved a swift resolution to the bad feelings. I longed for the hug, for the tears of joy and relief, and for the laughter that followed. I remember going to bed feeling safe. Everything was going to be all right, and I was the luckiest girl in the world. And when Matthew bounded through the door, peppermint ice cream all over his face, I went to hug him, but he had moved on.

"Mom, I'm too busy for this!" He ran to the backyard and out the back gate, searching for the source of a sound that only he could hear. Peter, still in his threadbare T-shirt, gave me a quick kiss and ran after Matthew.

Suddenly alone, I felt gripped with anxiety. I was haunted by the events of the afternoon—the look of disgust on the Asian woman's face, the police car in the driveway, the curious neighbors. I saw Matthew's tormented face, red from crying, and slick with a mixture of tears and slobber. I worried about Andy and John and knew they would hear from the kids at school. *There was a police car at your house! What happened?*

I knew that everything would not be all right.

And then the doorbell rang. It was my neighbor, Dori. She held a loaf of banana bread and before I could thank her, she gave me a hug.

CHAPTER 28

BEN

JUST WEEKS AFTER THE VISIT from Officer Jones, the summer of Matthew's fourteenth year began, and it was more than a handful. My mother was hospitalized again, and just like the summer before, I was driving back and forth to Carmel as much as I could while Peter juggled working at home with taking care of the boys. The final blow came when Chad, Matthew's paid companion, announced mid-August he could no longer help; he had gotten a full-time job.

The day before Matthew's first day of high school, I pushed open the door to Joe's Barbershop, the intense August heat on my back. Matthew trailed behind me, a big expectant smile on his face. He went straight for the lollipops on the counter, the ones you are supposed to get *after* the haircut.

Trips with Matthew to Joe, the barber, were a treat. They gave me a glimpse of "normal" as the two settled into a regular barbershop conversation that Joe modified to accommodate Matthew's interests.

Instead of "How about that ballgame," it was "Seen any poisonous plants lately?"

The barbershop was known and revered by the students at the local high school and the small private college nearby.

"Laura, you don't look so good," said Joe as he swept up from the last customer, and he was right. I looked like hell. I was tired and drawn, and I hadn't smiled in quite a while.

"Joe, you wouldn't know of any college students who are looking for, uh, babysitting jobs?"

I knew right away I should have used a different term.

"I'm not a baby! I'm a teenager and I don't need babysitters!" yelled Matthew.

"What I mean, Matthew, is a cool guy for you to hang out with. Like Chad."

"As a matter of fact, I know a really nice kid who's looking for work. He's a freshman at the college. He left his phone number on the bulletin board."

"Do you know anything about him?" I asked, holding up the scrap of paper with Ben's number on it.

"Not much. Seems nice enough," he replied. I envisioned a nerdy, scrawny, homesick kid who didn't have a social life and had decided he might as well babysit. I had no problem with that. I needed help.

Adolescence had kicked Matthew's impulsive behavior into high gear. He had become an escape artist, and I was often seen cruising around town in my minivan, anxiously searching for him. On these excursions, Matthew approached kids his age and begged them for friendship. He stood too close to girls and asked them if he could touch their hair. Faced with frequent police visits and neighborhood complaints, I would deliver flowers, bottles of wine, and cookies to those who had been upset by Matthew's shenanigans. Damage control had become my way of life.

I circulated brochures about autism to neighbors and law enforcement, who thought Matthew's behavior might be drug-related. Through it all, I worried about John and Andy, and about how Matthew's public scenes affected them. It was an unsettling time, and I was a wreck. Maybe this nice college boy could give me a hand.

I called Ben later that afternoon and left a message. His phone message said something like, "Yo, here comes the beep, you know what to do."

Maybe he wasn't such a nerd after all.

Ben called back the next morning and we arranged an interview for the next day. He sounded pretty normal on the phone. He mentioned that he played football for Saint Mary's College. *Hmm. . .*

One of my friends had stopped by to borrow a cup of sugar when the doorbell rang. I opened the door, and there he was—tall, blond, and unbelievably handsome. He kicked off his shoes as he entered the house and put his hand out to shake mine.

My friend stood there, her jaw on the floor.

"I'm Ben."

There was something in his eyes. It was a kind, sympathetic look that went straight to my heart. I knew nothing about this boy, or what kind of experience he had had, but I knew he was special.

"You don't have to take off your shoes," I said.

"I have two brothers. My mom always makes us take our

shoes off when we come in the house," he said, smiling.

Ben told me a little bit about himself. The sympathetic look turned sorrowful when he related that he had lost his father a few years back in a car accident, and that his mother was working hard to put her three college-age sons through school. He wanted to work as much as possible to lighten her load.

I, in turn, explained our situation to Ben, and he listened, nodding compassionately. He admitted that he knew nothing about autism, but was willing to learn. While I was telling Ben about some of Matthew's behaviors, and how best to handle them, Matthew emerged from his room, where he had been playing video games.

"Matthew, this is Ben," I said cautiously.

"He looks good," Matthew announced. Ben took Matthew out that very afternoon.

"Maybe you can play basketball or go for a hike or—"

"We'll be fine," said Ben reassuringly, and off they went in his blue pickup.

When they came back, Ben and Matthew looked tired and happy—almost fraternal. They had driven to Ben's dorm room to hang out, gone for pizza, and listened to music. Ben had shown Matthew the football stadium where he played and had introduced him to some of the guys on the team. They had gone to the pool and done cannonballs off the diving board. Guy stuff.

I handed Ben a generous check—bribery, of course—and asked if he would be interested in coming again. "Sure!" he answered enthusiastically. I gave him some information about autism to read over, and he went to find Matthew before he left.

"See ya tomorrow, my man," he said to Matthew, to which Matthew replied "That's cool" and swaggered out to see Ben zoom off in his truck.

Ben became a fixture at our house, coming three or four times a week to hang out with Matthew. John and Andy always ran out to meet Ben when his blue truck rolled into the driveway.

"Come look at my new guitar!" said Andy.

"I got a new video game!" John called. Ben spread the wealth of his presence, but he remained loyal to Matthew and heeded his call.

"Andy and John, I'm sorry to have to tell you this," said Matthew, "but Ben is my friend and not yours. We are very busy and don't want to be messed with. Let's go, Ben."

Not all of their outings together were totally fun and games, and Ben worked hard to manage Matthew's public peculiarities, coaching him gently through his social awkwardness. He explained that "How's it going?" works better than "Do you like me?" and showed him how to nod his head oh-so-slightly in the process.

I paid Ben well and often sent him home with clean laundry and a batch of cookies. But there were many times when he would drop Matthew off and refuse payment.

"It wouldn't be right, we had too much fun," he would say, even as I attempted to throw a wad of well-deserved money into his truck as he drove off laughing.

Matthew loved going to the mall with Ben. His charismatic good looks and great personality attracted an array of pretty, flirty girls who would otherwise run from Matthew's desperate, hungry gaze.

"Hey, man, you've gotta be cool. Don't stand so close. Girls don't like that."

Ben's influence on Matthew proved the phrase "The impact of the message depends on the messenger." He welcomed my calls for help when my message failed to make an impression.

Ben? Matthew's having a hard time understanding that he shouldn't put his arm around a girl he doesn't know. Can you talk to him?

Ben stayed connected to our family through his four years of college and even went on vacations with us during the summer to help with Matthew, but he always blended in like a member of the family.

"Four sons!" said a grandmotherly type one night when we all went out to dinner.

"Yeah," replied Ben, winking at me. "Isn't our mom the best?" I blushed.

At Ben's graduation, I overheard one of his uncles exclaim, "Now all he has to do is convince someone to hire him!"

But I knew that whoever was lucky enough to get him would *never* regret it.

CHAPTER 29

THE END OF THE LINE

EVEN BEFORE WE MET with the consultant who would help us find a school for Matthew, I was reassuring local police enforcement that he would be going to a residential school soon.

"How soon?" one officer asked.

Matthew was completing his freshman year of high school, a year with daily crises and few high points. He was in a special-education class that was new to the campus at our local high school, one for which parents had lobbied hard. The eight students in the program, all considered to be "SH," or severely handicapped, would spend most of their day in a dedicated classroom, but would be mainstreamed for one or two classes a day, depending on their abilities. They would also join the regular students for breaks and lunch with some supervision from peer tutors and instructional aides.

I knew it was going to be a challenging year when I went with another parent to meet the new teacher a few days before school started. We hoped she would be the dream teacher that would carry our teenagers through yet another difficult transition. We brought her flowers and assured her that we were there to support her, that we would do anything we could to make the new class work. We donated books and furniture and offered to work in the class for the first few weeks until instructional aides could be found. We could tell that the teacher thought we were too good to be true. Our optimism ebbed after we decided to pour our hearts out to this twenty-three-year-old first-time teacher who had never taught a special-education class. We were sharing the story of a short-lived middle-school teacher who had been a disaster.

"She didn't get it," I summarized.

"Get what?" replied the fresh new teacher who was about to take on eight severely handicapped and often unattractive teenagers.

"You know, get what the kids need, what it's like for the parents," my friend clarified.

"I don't understand. It should all be in the IEP what they need. What did you say about the parents?"

Uh-oh. She doesn't get it.

Looking back, I think even a perfect teacher would have had a hard time preventing the year from spinning out of control. Matthew's hormones were in high gear, and the bustling campus was teeming with, as Matthew would put it, "hot girls" and the cool guys that always attracted them.

Matthew was a mess. He distanced himself defiantly from the other students in the special class and often vanished, reappearing at the desk of a regular classroom, trying to blend in. He even changed his voice when he was discovered and asked to return to his class.

"I'm smart about physics," he would say in his lowest bass.

"Now leave me alone, I'm trying to work." One day a friend who was volunteering in the school library saw him being dragged back to class crying.

"It was so sad," she said. "He looked so hurt and humiliated."

One of the many calls I got from the principal's office came in March, a few months shy of the end of the school year. The story I got from the incensed vice principal was that Matthew had shoved a girl against the wall and hit her on the head. I was to meet the vice principal with Matthew in the office immediately. Driving like a maniac to the school, I knew there had to be more to the story.

I calmly picked up a blubbering Matthew from his class, as the teacher and aides looked at him with mild revulsion.

"Am I in trouble?" he wailed.

One of the teacher's aides stepped forward, her eyes darting back and forth between Matthew's and mine.

"You made a very bad choice. You'd better be careful about the choices you make."

Did she think what she was saying made any sense to Matthew?

I quickly ushered him out of the class. His sobs were out of control, and he couldn't get a breath. I found a spot out of view of the titillated students and teachers and got him to calm down in the way that always worked: "Awww…" with a rocking hug.

Finally he stopped crying, took a shuddering breath, and sat down on a patch of grass. I flashed back to the days when my boys were babies. They would always end a crying jag with the same heaving breath.

"Am I in trouble?" he asked again. With his face swollen from crying, he looked exhausted and utterly dejected.

"No, Matthew, you are not in trouble."

I meant what I said, knowing that his actions were understandable considering the environment I had placed him in. It had been my brilliant idea to help fashion a class for him in the middle of what for him was chaos.

"What really happened, honey? I know you wouldn't ever want to hurt anyone."

And he wouldn't. He had been known to strike out in frustration, only after biting his own hand to try to stop himself.

"We were all hanging out, and I saw Brad push a girl and hit her on the head and she liked it! She even hugged him! So I did it to Christina and she ran to the office crying!"

Matthew's brow crinkled up in distress again, and the tears returned. I put it all together. Brad must have shoved his girlfriend lightly and playfully, topping it off with a flirtatious tap on the head. He scored. Matthew, inspired by Brad's success, must have tried the same move, lacking his model's inherent finesse.

When we went to the principal's office, I offered my interpretation of the situation to the angry vice principal. After hearing my translation, she turned to Matthew, incredulous.

"You mean you hit Christina because you saw Brad hit Abby? Don't you know that you don't hit someone just because you see someone else do the same thing?"

I wished I had brought along a copy of the Web page from the National Autism Society that I kept for situations like this. I had a yellow pen in my purse to highlight the autistic behavior featured in the conflict, just like a salesman. I scribbled down the Web site as Matthew replied to her question.

"Abby liked it! She even gave Brad a hug!"

The vice principal shook her head disapprovingly. She didn't get it. I knew we weren't going to get anywhere, so I apologized and said we would talk to Matthew further about the situation during his suspension. On the way home, we stopped by the florist, bought flowers for Christina, and placed them on her doorstep, along with a note from me. I paused for a moment to dial the number of a school placement specialist on my cell phone, and then proceeded with the call as I drove off.

CHAPTER 30

THE SEARCH

AMY PRESTON'S NUMBER, jotted on the back of a bank deposit slip, had been stuffed in my wallet for three years. I had asked Rebecca if she knew anybody who *might* know about residential schools, just in case, *some*day. Today was that day. Amy Preston was a private high-school and college counselor who specialized in special-education placements.

I had always thought that the idea of sending Matthew away to school was cruel and ridiculous. I remember shaking my head judgmentally when I heard that a friend had sent her son with Down syndrome to boarding school.

"What kind of message does that send to her son?" I asked Peter. "'You are hard to handle, so we're sending you away.' The poor kid!" I'm embarrassed to admit that I continued my rant with other friends with disabled children.

"These kids are rejected every day of their lives! Can you imagine their own *families* rejecting them?"

"Oh, sure it would be a lot *easier* just to send Matthew somewhere."

The conversations evolved into fantasies about how much

easier family life would be if our kids went to a residential school.

"Just think! We could go to our kids' baseball games again!"

"And vacations! And dinner parties! We could have dinner parties!"

All the things so many people take for granted were a tremendous effort for us.

"But I would never do it!"

"Me, either!"

The longer the deposit slip hid in my wallet, however, the more reasonable the notion of a residential school became. With the increased frequency of unnerving incidents around town, the darkening tone of recent police visits, and Matthew's overzealous and misunderstood attempts at flirtation at school, I was tempted to skip the phone call and just show up at Amy Preston's office to get the ball rolling.

While Matthew and I waited for Amy in the reception room, a young man leafed earnestly through college brochures with his father, waiting to see one of Amy's colleagues. The father glanced over at us, trying to size up our situation. Both father and son wore khakis, polo shirts, and Top-Siders. The father had on one of those belts with whales embroidered on it.

How obnoxious, I thought. But then I looked over at Matthew in his bright yellow T-shirt, black shorts, dark socks, and sandals. He sat as far away from me as he possibly could, shooting me hateful looks.

I was in no position to judge. The man looked as if he might like to exchange pleasantries with me, but I kept my eyes glued to the magazine in front of me, knowing that the sound of my voice would send Matthew into a rage.

This was to be the second of three meetings with Amy. At the first, Peter and I had reviewed the recent events that had led us to consider a residential school for Matthew. Amy had already studied Matthew's school records and psychological evaluations. She had a few ideas for schools but needed to meet with Matthew first.

After a tense fifteen minutes in the reception area, Amy came out to usher us in.

"I'm not going to a new school!" Matthew bellowed. I felt the blood rush to my face and perspiration gush from my armpits. The father and his son looked up cautiously.

Amy's face, on the other hand, remained calm and businesslike.

"Why don't you and your mom come into my office?" she asked.

"My mother has to stay *here*!" he said, stomping his foot in the reception room.

"Your mother will come with us," said Amy assertively, and that was that.

During the brief meeting, Amy asked Matthew about his interests, what he liked to do when he wasn't in school, what he wanted to do for work when he was a man.

"I want to be the ice cream man in Carmel," Matthew said with conviction.

This was news to me.

Matthew tried to impress Amy with how smart he was. He told her that his balloons go *through* the clouds, not past the clouds. He asked her how many states she had been to. He told her that he was no one to be messed with. Through it all, Amy's expression remained earnest and professional. The paradox was more than my fragile state could take. I felt the giggles coming on and had to excuse myself.

Matthew and Amy emerged ten minutes later (*What in the world was going on in there?*), and we went home.

When Peter and I met with Amy the final time, she confirmed our belief that Matthew's needs were too great to be served in a public-school environment. His behavior at home and in the community indicated that a residential placement was needed for his safety and for his educational and personal growth.

As Amy was telling us what we had expected to hear, Peter and I were suddenly overcome with grief. We were really going to do this. It felt as if we were letting Matthew slip away after all the years of struggling to make things work.

"I know this is hard," Amy said, noticing our stricken expressions, "but once we find the right fit, your lives, the lives of your other two sons, and Matthew's will improve."

Amy had identified three schools that were a good fit for Matthew, all on the East Coast. The only potential good fit in California was a few hours away, but the students lived in group homes rather than on campus. Though we had never seen a group home, we worried. We imagined getting phone calls in the middle of the night—"Matthew has gotten out and we can't find him!" Given his history of disappearing from home in our own community, we needed the security of a school that was home.

Amy presented information about the three schools she had

in mind for Matthew. The first was a well-known center for autistic children in Boston. It had a great reputation, but Matthew would be one of the lower-functioning students. We thought that could be a good thing, that maybe he'd move up a notch. But Amy explained that the school was concerned about its lack of an appropriate peer group for Matthew. We appreciated this concern; we didn't want a replay of Matthew's lonely year at our local school.

The second school Amy had researched was one she hadn't been back to visit in a while, but she thought it was worth a look. Matthew would be one of the higher-functioning students, and the school focused primarily on vocational training. Peter and I felt that Matthew's program should be at least fifty percent academic, but we agreed to check the school out.

And then Amy told us about Camphill Special School.

I had heard about Camphill Communities. There was one in Santa Cruz, an hour and a half south of our Bay Area home. I knew that Camphill was a worldwide organization committed to building communities that nurture the growth and development of the disabled. I had thought of checking it out for Matthew when he was older, which at the time seemed very far in the future. Amy told us that many kids who start at Camphill Schools go on to live in Camphill Communities as adults.

We learned that Camphill Special School at Beaver Run was in Glenmoore, Pennsylvania, about forty-five miles west of Philadelphia. The students at the school, who range from age five to nineteen, live in an extended family with co-workers (often with their own children) and other volunteers in specially designed homes. The term "co-worker" is used to acknowledge the importance of working alongside people with disabilities to help them contribute as members of the community.

This seemed like a perfect formula for Matthew. He could live in a home with a family, along with other students, and have the benefit of living and learning beside peers without disabilities. The academic program, adapted from Waldorf education, focused on experimental learning and emphasized social, artistic, and practical skills. The program was supported by a variety of therapies available to help the student with his or her development.

"They have a spot for Matthew, and a terrific peer group for him to connect with."

Was there a catch? Please don't let there be a catch.

The only catch was that a meeting would need to take place soon, before someone else filled the spot.

It was May.

"We're going east for vacation in June. Is that soon enough?" Peter asked.

Are you nuts?

"I will be happy to fly back there tomorrow!" I offered, and I meant it.

Luckily, June was soon enough.

I thought I knew what I was looking for, but I had no idea what I was about to find.

CHAPTER 31

THE SCHOOL WE DIDN'T CHOOSE

PETER AND I BELIEVED THAT CAMPHILL, or a school just like it, sounded like the perfect place for Matthew, but we had to prove it to our local school district and the Regional Center of the Department of Developmental Services, which would share in the funding of a residential school placement for Matthew. Both asked us to consider some local alternatives.

None of the local alternatives was a residential school. Students attended the schools and lived in group homes.

"There is a school in a community just twenty-five minutes from your home," said Matthew's caseworker from the Regional Center. "The group home is just ten blocks away."

"Is it just me, or doesn't it seem crazy to even *consider* a group home for Matthew?"

I had nothing against group homes. I had visited a few and been very impressed. But for Matthew? Our main reason for choosing a residential school was that Matthew was known to wander from our home, and I was concerned that he was no longer safe, even in the community where he had grown up and was recognized. What would happen when he wandered from a group home in an unfamiliar neighborhood?

"You never know," said the caseworker. "And wouldn't it be nice to have Matthew so close?"

Sure! Then when he wandered away from the group home and was apprehended by the police, I could just drive over and pick him up.

Worried that our school district and the Regional Center might be inflexible, I called the special-education attorney that Amy Preston recommended and asked him what we should do.

"Go ahead and see what they have to offer," he advised. "Then you'll be able to explain why your choice is more appropriate. This is just part of the process."

I felt uneasy the day I went to visit the school, but I told myself to have an open mind. This might be a feasible option if Camphill didn't work out. The school was called, of all things, "A Better Place," and was located off a busy freeway in an area that looked like an industrial office park. I pulled into a diagonal parking place thinking I must have missed a turn somewhere; the building in front of me didn't appear to have any windows. But then I saw the "A Better Place" sign over a nondescript entrance, and I wandered in to find a long, dingy, empty hallway.

But all high-school hallways are dingy.

The old familiar lump found its way back to my throat as I thought of all the years I had helped carry Matthew through school and of all the gut-wrenching school meetings; of the psychologists, doctors, and behaviorists; and of the flowers and bottles of wine I had delivered to miffed neighbors and teachers. All that—for this? I was beginning to feel really sorry for myself when a when a boy about fifteen wearing baggy jeans and a

Rolling Stones T-shirt came to the rescue.

"Can I help you?" he asked, pushing his straight brown hair from his forehead. I couldn't tell the nature of this boy's disability. He had a kind, open face and sleepy blue eyes.

"By the way, I'm Jared, in case you wondered," he said, looking over his shoulder awkwardly as I followed him to the principal's office.

The principal sat hunched over her desk in a bay of cubicles, thumbing through a folder in front of her with a phone on one ear. She smiled and waved me in. Two boys, who looked a little older than Jared, waited sulkily before her, arms folded angrily across their chests.

I couldn't help but like this woman. She was in her mid-forties and looked tired and drawn, a look I had been featuring lately. Her hair hung straight to her shoulders and was the same light beige as her skin; her blue eyes peeked through white eyelashes. I could tell she was a kind soul who understood the road that had led me here. She introduced me to the sullen boys before sending them off to work at an auto shop, one of the many vocational training units that the school offered. As they sauntered off, I remarked that these boys looked pretty normal.

"Most of our students have mild to moderate learning disabilities and behavioral issues. About half of them live in group homes in the area."

"Hmmm, Matthew is autistic. Do you have any autistic students?"

"No, we don't, but I'm sure we could work something out."

I'm through with working things out. I need a place where things are already worked out.

"Is he high-functioning?" she asked.

"Not nearly as high-functioning as the students I've met so far."

The principal glanced through a folder marked with Matthew's name.

"Well, I think it all depends on what other students we get for the fall. We might have to modify our program to accommodate him. How about a tour?"

We walked down the hall I decided wasn't that dingy after all, and we stepped into a geometry class where eight boys and two girls sat at desks working on a problem while the teacher wandered around the room helping them. A few of them were leaning back with their legs outstretched and looked a lot older and more physically mature than Matthew. Looks can be deceiving, but this group appeared to be communicating and functioning at a much higher level than Matthew was capable of.

There had been a time when I thought being with higher-functioning students would accelerate Matthew's achievement and improve his behavior. I had since learned that Matthew couldn't be forced, that doing so would make him an anxious, lonely mess.

After the brief tour, the principal walked me out to my car where we talked for a few minutes. I glanced around the outside of the school and cringed, thinking of Matthew impulsively running into the busy street that bordered it. The principal handed me directions to the group home.

"Call me next week and we'll schedule some time to show Matthew around."

We both knew I wouldn't.

I followed the directions to the group home, wondering whether there was a decent bottle of wine at home in the fridge. I noticed a childcare center on my left as I approached the corner where the home stood. Not good. One of Matthew's obsessions these days was babies. He had the habit of asking mothers, "When was the last time you changed your baby's diaper?" or worse, "Can I watch you change your baby's diaper?" He had been known to steal diapers from the homes of my friends to put on his stuffed bear, Bill. But that's another story.

The group home stood on the corner of a neighborhood consisting of ranch homes in shades of brown, beige, and olive green with contrasting shutters and the occasional wagon wheel in front. There were a few for rent signs on the street, but the homes looked well-maintained. I walked up the cracked concrete path that led to the door and knocked.

No answer.

I peeked in the window and saw that the home was in some stage of remodeling, with a stepladder in the entryway and a roll of linoleum jutting out from what must have been the kitchen. I heard a car door slamming behind me, then turned and saw a well-dressed woman also in her mid-forties sitting in her silver BMW, finishing a phone call and applying lipstick.

"So sorry I'm late!" she said, waving her cell phone. "My son is locked out of the house and I had to have my ex-husband drive over with the key."

Sorry I'm early. I'm a little depressed about the group-home scene and can't wait to get the hell out of here.

"Hello," said the woman, "I'm one of the owners of the home. You must be Matthew's mom!"

That's me.

"Your timing is perfect. One of our boys is leaving to move into another home around the corner," she said as she opened the front door.

"Do you live here with the kids?"

"No, we have staff that rotates. George and Paul are usually here nights, then Rosalie and Pat share days. You'll meet Rosalie a little later."

"Is there a lot of turnover in the house?"

"The kids or the staff?" asked the owner.

"Uh, both, I guess."

"Well, it all depends on the kids and how they get along with each other and the staff. When things aren't working we make changes."

I felt a pit in my stomach and decided to change the subject.

"Wow! An aquarium!" I said, walking into one of the four small bedrooms.

"Oh, well, the aquarium is leaving with Bobby tomorrow."

I stepped cheerfully over the rolls of linoleum and carpet remnants, a fake smile plastered on my face as we wandered through the house, ending in the kitchen and family room with a TV and video game console in the corner. I felt my face twitch— muscle fatigue from all the smiling. If I started to cry, how in the world would I hide it?

"Does Matthew have any hobbies?"

Yes, he likes to dress stuffed bears in diapers and he loves babies.

"He loves landscaping."

"Great," she said, walking me out back. There was a nice yard with a lawn and flowers bordering it. "He can be in charge of the garden."

"Can I ask a question? Matthew likes to wander, and I worry about that."

The woman looked puzzled.

"What do you mean. . . wander? Does he like to go for walks?"

"Well, sort of, and he's autistic, so sometimes he'll say inappropriate things to people and make them angry."

"Well, I guess one of the staff will just have to keep an eye on him."

I did my best to wrap things up. I had seen enough to "prove why our choice was more appropriate," but instead of feeling vindicated, I felt sad and empty.

"Oh my gosh, what time is it? I need to pick up the kids from school!"

At this moment, I couldn't wait to see Matthew and give him a hug. On the way out, Rosalie was on her way in. She had come just to meet me, Matthew's mother.

"What do you think?" asked Rosalie proudly.

"It's all wonderful," I said, finally caving in with a shaky voice. I figure it was OK to sound emotional. It could mean whatever they wanted it to mean.

"Awww," said Rosalie, "it's hard to let go, isn't it?"

"Yes, it is," I said, wiping my eyes. But letting go wasn't the problem. Trusting someone to nurture Matthew and keep him safe was.

I drove home in a daze. What would I do if no other school would take him? Maybe I could make things work in our community, hire full-time help to police his wanderings. Maybe I could hire a mentor he admired to go to school with him.

Maybe Camphill will take him.

THE ROAD TO THE
FUTURE

CHAPTER 32

BEAVER RUN

PETER AND I LEFT with Matthew before sunlight hit the lake in New Hampshire, where we'd been on vacation. Andy and John stayed behind with Peter's family, who were vacationing with us. We had a six-hour drive ahead of us—our destination, Camphill Special School at Beaver Run, Pennsylvania.

Driving with Matthew had always been difficult. He demanded silence—no radio, no conversation; even a cough or a sneeze would set him off. He said he needed silence because he was "knowing something" and didn't want his thoughts to be interrupted. Today's drive was heartbreaking, as Matthew alternated between tears and desperate conversations. . . with himself.

"We're just looking at this school, Matthew, you don't have to go there. I know! Besides, they actually think you're a good kid at home. They will surely take you back."

Hearing his mutterings, I wanted desperately to soothe his anguish, but I couldn't. It was clear that school and life in our community were not working for him, and he sensed that. Still, he wanted so badly to fit in. And here he was, three thousand miles from where he imagined he belonged, feeling rejected and abandoned, longing for a life he could never have.

Everything rode on this visit. The school had a spot for Matthew based on the application and the information that Amy Preston had supplied, but a visit would determine whether Camphill and Matthew were right for each other. It was June, and Camphill was both our favorite and our only decent choice.

In the prior week, I had made a trip to the Boston area to check out Plan B with disheartening results. The school, which looked great in brochures and on Web sites, was run down and surrounded by four busy streets lined with strip malls, gas stations, and a grammar school. My first thought when I had approached the school was, what if Matthew gets out? He'll wander over to the grammar school, as he had at home, and frighten young girls with inappropriate questions.

Later, the director of the school would assure me that the police were "pretty good" about finding and returning kids. The same director asked me, "What causes autism?" During the tour of the dormitories, I noticed that there were several televisions in each of the rooms.

"Oh," explained the director, "each child is allowed to bring his own TV and game system for 'down time.'"

"Wow" was all I could manage while we toured the dreary dining hall and the cage-like basketball courts. Both reeked suspiciously of Lysol.

On the way out, the director told me we would need to schedule a two-week evaluation period in the fall; if it went well, Matthew could enroll in the spring. Had this been a desirable choice, I would have stomped my feet and explained that there must have been a misunderstanding; Amy Preston had assured us a spot in the fall. Instead, I drove back to the lake in New Hampshire, feeling more desperate than I ever had in my life. Our local school would not take him back and our other choices looked dismal. God, please let Camphill accept him. Please let Camphill be what it *claims* to be.

As we followed the road leading to Camphill, Matthew began to look at his surroundings with interest. It was beautiful. Camphill is in rural Chester County, which borders Lancaster County and the Amish Country. The rolling green landscape featured farmhouses and ponds with bales of hay dotting the fields.

We crossed a narrow bridge over a rocky creek, and saw a sign: "Camphill Special School—A Children's Village."

A short distance down the wooded driveway, a clearing revealed the first building in the village—a large stone house with blue and white flowers cascading from window boxes. When we got out of the car, a cat that had been napping on the sunny porch rose to rub against my leg. The door of the house was opened, and we were greeted by the smell of fresh paint. We stepped bravely through the door and found ourselves in a sunny room with several pairs of shoes lined up along the wall. There was a large kitchen through an arched doorway where two young men were busy rolling paint on the ceiling, laughing as they worked. "What's going on here?" Matthew moaned loudly.

The young men, startled by Matthew's wailing, burst into laughter.

"What's so funny?" Matthew yelled.

"Nothing, nothing, you just scared us!" they laughed. "Can

we help you?" Both young men spoke with an accent.

They were Christophe and Daniel. They told us they were students from Germany who were taking a few years off to work at Camphill. Christophe had already worked in the community a year, and Daniel had just started the previous week.

"It is hard work," Christophe said proudly, "but I love it."

"Speaking of hard work," I said, glancing at Matthew, who was seething, "we'd better get going."

"I'll be right there," Peter said.

I waited on the sunny porch with my poor tortured son as Peter quickly toured the rest of the house. He joined us a few minutes later, looking exhilarated.

While we waited to meet with the admissions director, we wandered up the road to get a look at the place we had heard so much about, with Matthew growling in protest behind us. We could see five large, attractive redwood homes up the hill, scattered in the midst of wooded pastures with horses and chickens meandering about.

The admissions director, Bernie, found us as we were luring Matthew up to the barn. He looked like an aging hippie, with his worn flannel shirt, Birkenstocks, and scruffy beard. His calm and gentle manner stood in stark contrast to Matthew's contrary bearing and our own frantic attempts to assure Bernie that Matthew was actually thrilled to be here, but was tired from the long drive.

As we began our tour, Bernie tried to lighten things up by pointing out a fat little toad to Matthew, who promptly stomped on it and fell into a heap, crying.

It was not the typical impulsive move that said, "I'm trying to connect with you."

Peter and I were mortified. I looked warily at Bernie, searching for reassurance. What was that expression on his face? Horror? Compassion? Was he wondering how he could get rid of us? I thought, he must be used to impulsive behavior, but clearly this murderous outburst had not been a good icebreaker. I decided that now was not the best time to mention that Matthew was not particularly fond of animals.

"This place is weird! Can we just go home? I'm sure they'll take me back! I promise I'll be a good kid!"

My chest tightened with anxiety. "Matthew, you are *already* a *great* kid. Some people at home just had a hard time understanding that!" I had used this reassurance with him before, and his chin trembled in appreciation today as it had before.

As we continued on the tour, Matthew lagged behind, and Bernie shared his concern that if Matthew didn't want to be here, perhaps we shouldn't force him. While we did our best to convince Bernie that there was nowhere else in the world but here, and please, please, he'll get used to it, we saw Bernie smile and nod in Matthew's direction. Our first moment of Camphill magic was in the works.

Ten yards down the hill from where we were begging, Matthew stood mesmerized as a man riding a John Deere tractor mowed the pasture while two young men carried bales of hay and piled them next to the barn. One appeared to have severe cerebral palsy, even worse than Uncle Russell, and the other looked stoic and repeated the phrase "I'm sorry, Joe" over and over. I had worried how Matthew, who thought of himself as a regular guy, would feel in the company of young men like these who were severely disabled.

"We are a community with diverse abilities that work well together," pointed out Bernie. "It's hard for parents to see that at first, but it is a philosophy that we impress on the students from the beginning."

The man on the tractor jumped down and handed Matthew a fistful of grass and invited him to feed a horse that was ambling by. Matthew acquiesced, but the moment he saw that we were watching, the magic fizzled, and he sulked loudly and dramatically. Peter coaxed Matthew to join us up the hill to meet Matthew's prospective teacher, Guy.

"You must be the Shumakers!" said a short, athletic-looking blond man with glasses, a British accent, and a huge smile. He wore cargo shorts, a T-shirt, and hiking boots. He stuck his hand out to shake mine and saw me roll my eyes and gesture to Matthew, who was sitting on the dirt path behind us, looking disgruntled. Guy let out a huge belly laugh and the reassurance that I was looking for earlier enveloped me.

"Having a little trouble, are we?" Guy said, his eyes dancing. I could tell that he was the kind of person who drew out the best in everyone.

"Let's get out of here!" Matthew wailed. "It looks bad!"

"I know how you feel, chap!" Guy chuckled, while he studied our weary faces.

Matthew glared at him dramatically and looked down at the dirt path again.

"Good luck!" said Bernie, making his way back toward the carcass of the dead toad. "Come on by the office on the way out."

Was this a good sign or a bad sign?

Peter and I were tormented by the prospect of this dream slipping away, brutally sabotaged by the very person who stood to gain so much from it. Guy could sense that. He waved us forward to a spot where we could keep our eye on Matthew but talk without being heard. He told us he wasn't worried about Matthew's contrary behavior—it was to be expected. Peter and I looked at each other and sighed with relief.

"What do you want for your son?" Guy asked us.

We told Guy our story—from the early days of innocence through the highs and lows of special education to Matthew's recent troubles at school and in the community. We told him about our family and of our struggle to raise Matthew while meeting the needs of our other two boys. I told him that I feared for Matthew's safety in our community and that I knew Matthew felt pushed aside by his former school and by the kids he imagined to be his friends. Guy listened intently, glancing intermittently at Matthew, still sitting in the dirt—a lost fifteen-year-old with few choices.

"I've seen a lot of kids like Matthew," said Guy, "and believe me, we have just the right program for him. We can really make a difference." There was such passion and conviction in his response that Peter and I were overwhelmed with emotion and gratitude. Here was someone who was willing to take on a tremendous challenge and yet who acted as if we were giving him a gift.

"It will be a privilege to work with your son," Guy continued confidently.

Guy explained that Matthew would be in a class with eight other students, mostly boys, and told us about a few of his prospective classmates. The students had a range of disabilities, but two of them, both boys, were also autistic and functioning on a level similar to Matthew's. Class was between 8:30 and noon, and afternoons were spent working on the land and in other vocational training activities.

"As you know, we use the Waldorf curriculum. We'll start with a unit on Greek mythology, and follow that with a unit on space. Math and reading are incorporated into each day's work."

My head was spinning. *How in the heck does he do it?* I could tell by his confident manner that this man *finds* a way.

"And explain to us again," I asked. "What is the living situation like?"

"I'll use my house as an example. Ani and I are the house-holders, and we live here with our two boys. Eight students live in the home with us, as do co-workers, as many as one for each student, depending on the nature of the students' disabilities. The students do their own laundry, help with cooking and other household chores. We always manage just fine," he said with a smile.

"If Matthew is accepted, will he live in your house?" Peter asked.

"No, Matthew will live in a house with students his age. We

like the students to live with their peer group. But I look forward to teaching him."

Was this a done deal? He makes it sound like a done deal.

Guy took us on a tour of his house, which was the largest at Beaver Run.

For the first time since Matthew was diagnosed, I felt the sheer joy of finally having a promising path to follow and a solid reason for hope.

———————

The rest of our visit to Camphill was a blur. I remember that Peter and I were shaking with excitement and relief, and that Matthew calmed down and admitted that he liked the school, countering quickly with "if I needed a new school, but since I *don't*—" We hadn't expected him to sign on right away. At least this was something.

"Why don't you go on to the office and talk with Bernie?" Guy suggested. "Matthew and I will be fine." He followed Matthew, who had wandered down to the field that had captivated him earlier.

"I think he's in!" I said as we walked anxiously toward the office, covered with goose bumps.

———————

"Well, what do you think?" said Bernie.

"What do *we* think?" Peter asked nervously. "It's what *you* think that we're worried about."

"Well, we have a spot for Matthew. Are you interested?" he

asked with a broad grin. "Let me give you some paperwork."

Peter and I floated back up the hill and found Matthew and Guy sitting on the front porch drinking lemonade.

"I like this place," said Matthew, "but I'm not going here."

Oh, yes you are.

"Well, I sure hope you change your mind," said Guy, smiling.

"I might" was Matthew's response. We thanked Guy enthusiastically and were on our way.

As we drove away from Camphill, elated, I realized that I would soon be able to answer the questions that had been haunting me for so many years.

"Where will he live? What will he do?"

He'll live and learn at Camphill Special School. That will be the beginning of his road into adulthood.

CHAPTER 33

MISSING MATTHEW

ANDY SKIPPED AHEAD OF ME with his fresh haircut and new Quiksilver T-shirt. He tumbled into a cluster of exuberant but nervous freshmen outside the high-school gym as upperclassmen clapped and chanted, music blaring. It was orientation day. I was in a state—excited for Andy, but consumed with the memory of the last time I had seen Matthew, standing on the front lawn of his new home at Camphill just a few days before, looking abandoned. His parting words to us had been, "I'm a regular kid, aren't I?" Had he gotten his way, he would have been a sophomore at our local school.

When it was time to get to the business of filling out forms and taking pictures for student body cards, I felt a tug on my sleeve. It was the mother of one of Andy's friends. This woman had the reputation for knowing all.

"I hear you sent Matthew away to school," she said coldly.

"Yeah, it's hard, but I think it will be good for him in the long run."

"Well, I think it's sad," she said, then turned and walked away.

I raced around and paid for books and registration fees with

Andy running behind me, knowing I was distressed. I kept my chin to my chest, eyes down. Only a few of my good friends could tell that something was wrong as tears stained my beet-red face and light blue T-shirt.

"I'm fine," I lied to Andy with my best fake smile. "Go ahead and talk to your friends. I'll meet you in the car."

Plastic smile still planted on my face, I ran to the car, fell in, and sobbed for what felt like hours. It was the first time I had cried since leaving Matthew at Camphill just two days ago. Andy was right behind me and sat next to me as I wept, patting my back lightly and giving me sips from his water bottle.

"You did the right thing, Mom," he said. "That lady wouldn't have said that if she knew what you've been through."

Parents and students were still streaming by as I took a breath and started the car. I glanced up and saw Ellen, another town busybody, striding toward us.

"Hurry!" Andy yelled, and we took off laughing, leaving poor Ellen looking gypped. On the way home, Andy and I imagined her with the phone to her ear, spreading the drama.

"She was crying really hard and wouldn't talk to anyone. Then she got in her car and cried some more. I bet they're having marital/financial/health problems! I'll find out and get back to you!"

It hadn't been easy to leave Matthew at Camphill, and I was exhausted from the turbulent summer, the constant tension. There were rages and slamming doors, police visits and angry calls. Matthew tore desperately around town in his attempt to leave an indelible impression on our community "in case I decide to go to that school in Pennsylvania." He did so by, among other things, approaching strangers, mostly prepubescent girls and their mothers, with inapt questions.

"How old are you? Do you think I'm nice?"

He got hold of the high school directory and frantically called everyone in it.

"I'll see you in September!" he'd say.

"Great!" was the response, though most had no idea who was calling.

"See, Mom and Dad? Everyone wants me to stay!"

He wrote a letter to the principal promising that he would be a good kid and asked us to do the same, not knowing that we had spent countless hours advocating for his transfer. We explained the logic of the move to him consistently and calmly.

"You are a great kid, but they don't have a program for you at your old school."

We cited examples of kids he knew who were going to private schools. But nothing we said soothed him. He felt he was being shoved out of his home and community.

With the end of the summer in sight, I felt more and more like a crazed animal, waking with a start in the morning, devouring a bowl of cereal and chugging coffee. But I stayed focused on Matthew and handled his daily flare-ups with remarkable calm. It was a comment from a specialist who had treated Matthew over the years that tripped me up. I had sent her a note asking her to send some medical records to Camphill.

"I'm surprised that you would send Matthew so far away!" she said. "Have you truly examined all of the alternatives? And this place Camphill? I've never heard of it!"

Overwrought and guilt-ridden, I drove Matthew, Andy, and John to the pediatrician for their annual checkups and shared the deflating conversation with him. Dr. Oken had taken care of the boys since the tender years when Matthew was first diagnosed, and he had always praised me for balancing Matthew's care with that of the other boys. But now we could see that the balancing act had become impossible.

"You know you are doing the right thing for Matthew," he said. "Let's not forget that you have two other wonderful boys." I looked at Andy and John giggling as they tested each other's reflexes, knees flying up dramatically, and I smiled. To hell with the critics. Sending Matthew to Camphill was not just an option—it was a necessity.

I wasn't prepared for the way I felt when Peter and I returned after taking Matthew to Pennsylvania. I had assumed it would take a day or two to decompress after the tumultuous summer, but then—with Matthew well taken care of and the other boys at school—I'd finally be able to enjoy the luxury of time alone in the house. I imagined that I'd reconnect with friends over lunch and at the gym. The strain that had aged my face would fall away, and I would look and feel rested and serene.

"Don't bet on it," Rebecca had said. "The days and weeks ahead will be some of the toughest of all."

I didn't believe her. I'd be fine. Heck, I'd be more than fine.

But Rebecca was right. Without the child who had required ninety-nine percent of my time and energy, I felt scattered and aimless. The anxious summer had drained my energy and confidence and battered my identity.

I had been the primary Matthew caregiver and expert for fifteen years. I had known exactly how to hold him when he fussed as a baby, and I knew the story behind every scar and broken bone. I was the only one who knew how to calm him down during an adolescent autistic meltdown. But now I felt stripped of my badge.

How can I be so sure they know what they are doing?

It seemed unnatural, even selfish, to fill the time Matthew's absence granted me with luxurious activities such as seeing friends for lunch, relaxing in the garden, or even doing a load of laundry without interruption.

The phone rang just as Andy and I were on our way out the door for orientation. It was one of my more clueless friends, Janine.

"Has Matthew left yet? Good! You must be so relieved! He doesn't come home till Thanksgiving? *Thank God!*"

"Yeah, well, I gotta run" was all I could manage. As I hung up, I heard her say, "Oh, I didn't mean it *that* way!"

After Andy and I returned from the scene of my public breakdown, the phone was ringing. Probably Janine again.

"Hello, Laura? This is Andrea at Camphill." Andrea was Matthew's housemother. I panicked.

"Is everything OK? Did something happen?" I asked.

"Oh no," she laughed, "things are going well here. I am really enjoying Matthew, but I have some questions about him, and I hope you can help me."

My heart jumped. Yes! I can help! What do you need to know?

What are his favorite foods? she asked. Does he like music? How do you reward him for good behavior? He has been teasing his roommate relentlessly.

That's a good sign. At least I know he's feeling like himself.

Any ideas? The rash that was on his hands seems to have cleared up since you left, and he is sleeping well. We are enjoying him so much! Andrea told me that Matthew liked to watch her son, Joe, who was eighteen, work in the greenhouse and that they got along well.

"He tells my son that they are 'like regular guys together.'"

I felt overwhelmed with joy and relief. Matthew was still far away, but he was safe, he was happy, and he was appreciated.

We talked for almost a half hour, mother to mother, and I told her to call me *any* time. It occurred to me that I had felt I was a failure as a mother because I couldn't fix Matthew. But now Andrea was acknowledging that Matthew was a puzzle, and that we needed each other to figure him out and help him grow.

"May I say hello to Matthew?"

"He's right here."

"Hi, Matthew!"

"Hi, Mom. I'm very busy right now. Joe and I are doing something very important."

"I know. I just wanted to hear your voice," I said, choking up. "I miss you, Matthew, and I love you *so* much."

I could tell he was smiling.

"That's nice."

CHAPTER 34

BOUNCING BACK

"MOM? CAN I ASK A HUGE FAVOR?" Andy's thirteen-year-old voice cracked from low to high. "Can you help me clean up the house real quick? Luke and Greg are on their way over."

The last time Andy had had friends over was four years ago, when Matthew had blasted the garden hose through the window and drenched the group of nine-year-old friends who were playing Battleship. Even with Matthew three thousand miles away at a residential school, Andy had been nervous about having friends over again. He was out of practice.

"Tell you what. You work on your room, and I'll do the rest," I said, already heaving the mountain of laundry off the living room couch and carrying it to my bedroom closet. I flipped on the oven in the kitchen. Maybe I'd whip up a batch of cookies, or would that make it look as if we were trying too hard?

Within minutes, the clutter of the house was hurled into my room, the house was vacuumed and the toilets cleaned. The scent of Lysol hung in the air from a quick wet-mop job when the doorbell rang.

"Hi, guys!" I said, grinning like a modern June Cleaver. "He's back in his room!"

They followed the sound of the electric guitar. Andy must have picked it up when he heard the doorbell ring, trying to act nonchalant.

I hid the mop and ran out to the yard to pick some roses. What am I thinking? These are boys! But maybe their mothers do flowers. What the hell.

After cutting a random assortment of roses, daisies, and salvia, I wondered if we had anything to eat. I ran to the kitchen, dropped the flowers in a vase, and threw open the cupboards. We had cereal, a few stale goldfish. No soda, only grape juice and milk. Popcorn? No. Better whip up those cookies. But first I had better change my shirt .Andy thinks I look good in the blue V-neck. Running to my room, I hear the boys laughing when I pass Andy's door, and my heart swells, my face warms. I hop over the laundry in my room and pull on the blue V-neck, brush my hair, put on some lipstick. I look fleetingly in the mirror. *Not bad.*

Rushing back to the kitchen, I pull out the mixer and throw the ingredients together. Within thirty-five seconds, the dough is ready, and I pull out the cookie sheets.

Oh, no! Here they come! I try to look casual as I slap the dough onto the pans.

"Cookie dough!" crows Andy as the three slide into the kitchen. "My mom makes the best cookies. Can we have some dough?"

"Sure!" I say casually. This is not the time to give a salmonella sermon. Luke wanders into the family room and takes in our garden.

"Ooooo, Andy, your backyard is awesome!"

Andy flashes me a glorious, grateful smile. His eyes are shining. It's almost more than I can take. I hope his friends don't notice my goose bumps.

"Let's go, guys," says Greg.

"Mom, we're walking downtown. See you later."

"Thank you, Mrs. Shumaker," they say, dipping their hands once more into the bowl of dough.

"Have fun!"

And they are out the door.

Andy runs back in, shouting to his friends that he forgot something. "Thank you sooo much, Mom. You were perfect!"

I quickly wipe away the tear that's made its way down to my chin while Andy squeezes me in a hug. He grabs his Cal baseball cap and runs out, forgetting to close the door in his exuberance. I close the door, pause, and put the cookies in the oven.

They'll be back.

CHAPTER 35

THE BIRTHDAY

IT WAS THE FIRST YEAR I would not be with Matthew on his birthday. He was turning sixteen and completing his first year at Camphill.

Birthdays since his autism diagnosis had been difficult. They coincided with Matthew's IEP, a yearly meeting that outlined his educational and behavioral goals for the year to come.

The IEP reviewed his progress in meeting the goals set in the prior year. There was always a discussion of his IQ and his actual grade level—both low. These meetings were devastating to me. I worried about them for weeks before, cried during, and went into a decline after.

It was always difficult to rally for a birthday party, and I felt heartbroken with regret every time Matthew blew out his candles. I couldn't help but envision what the day might be like were he not autistic.

While I would be spared the trauma of Matthew's sixteenth birthday, I was also despondent that I wouldn't be with him to share this landmark. Other friends with sixteen-year-olds were giddily planning Sweet Sixteen parties and trips to the DMV, and I told myself that *thank God* Matthew wasn't here, aware of being excluded from the parties and the driving. But I wanted to do something special for him.

I decided to treat Matthew and his housemates to dinner at his favorite restaurant, and to have sixteen balloons delivered to him. Matthew loved balloons. They were given to him as a reward for good behavior, and he still liked to attach signs to the balloons and let them go, watching them till they disappeared into the horizon. As he watched them, he hopped and flapped his hands, smiling and laughing as the balloons floated upward past trees and rooftops. He imagined who else saw the balloons and where they landed. It was quite an event and, admittedly, a great way to kill time on days that seemed to go on forever.

I called David, who was in charge of the house where Matthew lived with eight other teenage students, and explained my plan for Matthew's birthday, thinking he would be thrilled with my benevolence. He thanked me for the generous dinner offer, but the balloons wouldn't be necessary. He's sixteen years old, David said, and too old for balloons.

Good grief. He's autistic. Give the kid a break.

"David, come *on*. He always gets balloons on his birthday."

David paused before telling me what I needed to hear. "You have got to stop treating him like a child," he said. "No more toys and jellybeans. The Pokémon cards have got to go. When he comes home for the summer, put the Legos away and give him chores. Make sure he does them. He is a teenager."

David was right. He could tell that I was embarrassed for babying Matthew, and he sympathized. It is a pattern that parents of disabled teens fall into while trying to cope with this transition, difficult even in the best of circumstances. What better way to comfort a kid who lives with daily disappointment and loneliness than buying him a red balloon, an ice cream cone, or renting the latest Winnie the Pooh movie? David said a better way was to let them give of *themselves*. They have spent their lives being cared for. The power of being able to give in return is as rewarding as it is restorative.

"He's not going to like this," I warned, feeling guilty about making David's work even harder than it already was.

"We know, and we are ready to help him," assured David.

When Peter and I called Matthew on his birthday, he cried, "You said I would get balloons!"

"You're a big guy now," said Peter, choking up as Matthew sobbed. "Too old for balloons." What we both would have given to snap our fingers and be there to give him a hug.

I called David the day after Matthew's birthday. He reported that Matthew had cried a lot on his birthday, mourning the loss of his departing childhood and fearing what would replace it.

The following evening I called Matthew, prepared for another heart-wrenching conversation.

"Hi, Mom! Today I was very busy," he said, sounding exhilarated. "I have a very important job now. I work in the vegetable garden with David!"

He went on to tell me of all the equipment he had used, and how important it was to take care of his garden tools. He asked me to hand the phone to his dad, who could tell that the news was good by the tears in my eyes and the smile on my face.

CHAPTER 36

A GREAT LOSS

"GRANDMA, I DON'T LIKE YOU TO WEAR THAT," Matthew said, standing in the doorway of my parents' bedroom. He was referring to the plastic tube that cradled Mom's face, pushing oxygen through her nose. It was the last day of August 2002, just before Matthew was to return to Camphill for his second year.

"Matthew, you can come over and sit next to me. I'll show you how this works."

He plopped onto the bed next to my mom and listened as she explained how her lungs were tired, and how the plastic tube carried oxygen that kept her going.

"I don't like it, it looks bad," said Matthew. "I like you better the other way. I like it better when you're not in bed all the time."

"Matthew," I started, but Mom signaled that she could handle it.

"Here," she said, pulling the plastic tubing from her nose, just for a few seconds. "Is that better?"

Matthew's face exploded with joy.

"Hi, Grandma!" he said, holding her too tight, but not tight enough.

Just one month later, with Matthew safely back at school, my father called at 3:10 in the afternoon, and I knew, because we always talked at 8:30 a.m., and then at 5:20 p.m., right before Tom Brokaw.

"Mama died," he said. I told him I'd be right there.

I drove to Carmel calmly, yet tearfully, calling people from the road to share the news. Everyone expected it, but no one could believe it. Only 71 when she died, she never complained during her steady decline. Instead, she remarked daily about how lucky she was.

Dad had taken care of my mother cheerfully and tirelessly. His family and friends encouraged him to get help, a night nurse or an aide, but he refused, and somehow survived the years of constant caring, lifting, and lack of sleep. When my mother was discouraged, he would take her face in his hands and tell her he loved her. Even when she was at her worst, Dad took her to get her nails done or her hair styled, or out to lunch at a favorite spot. He made sure her lipstick was always nearby; he prepared and presented her meals with flair. She continued to laugh at his jokes, and he at hers, his eyes glistening with grief.

By the time I got to Carmel, Mom's body had been taken away, and Dad was leafing through his address book calling one name after the other.

"Joannie? Phil Bowhay. Susie passed away this morning. I know you did, she loved you too."

My dad was so distraught that I didn't dare shed a tear or cave in to my grief, and I took over the phone calls when it got to be too much for him. But there was one phone call that neither of us had the courage to make that day.

"When are you going to tell Matthew?" Dad asked. "You've got to call Matthew."

It was bedtime in Pennsylvania, so I decided to put the call off until the next morning. I shared the news with Matthew's house-father, David, who encouraged me to call early the next day so that Matthew's housemates could say a prayer for my mother at the morning meeting.

"Hi, Matthew. It's Mom."

"Why are you calling?" he asked calmly.

"Matthew, I have some very sad news to tell you. Grandma died yesterday."

"She died?" he yelled. He dropped the phone and wailed, "My Grandma died! Oh my God! I loved my Grandma so much!"

"Matthew?" I tried yelling into the mouthpiece loud enough that he would hear me and pick up the phone again.

"MATTHEW?" I started crying, sobbing for the first time since I'd heard the news myself.

Matthew picked up the phone again and started to ask questions. When did she die? Tell me everything. What was she doing when she died? What did Grandpa do when she died? What was I doing when she died? Was I just kidding, and was she actually alive? No, I cried, I'm not kidding.

"What was the last thing she said?" he asked tearfully. I turned to my father.

"Dad," I sobbed, "Matthew wants to know what Mom's last words were."

Dad took the phone and said, "Matthew? The last thing Grandma said was 'I sure am proud of Matthew. I sure love him.'"

CHAPTER 37

BACK TO SCHOOL

IT WAS BACK TO SCHOOL NIGHT at the beginning of Andy's sophomore year in high school, and Peter and I couldn't wait. We had had so much heartache in the past year with Mom's illness and death. Since Andy was a great student and well-loved by his teachers, we knew we were in for a much-needed upbeat evening.

We bounced from class to class, casting knowing looks at the other parents of smart children, exhilaration mounting as we proudly introduced ourselves to teachers.

When we sat down in Andy's French class, I glanced at the father sitting in the desk next to me.

"Laura?"

I remembered him as Steve; his son George and Matthew had been on a soccer team together back in kindergarten. Steve was a good-looking guy who was aging well. He worked out and wanted you to know it. Dressed in worn Oxford polo shirts and jeans, he wore preppy framed glasses, and his longish hair was graying just right. Matthew's time on the team with Steve's son had been his last experience on a mainstream team. Matthew always wanted to throw the ball over the fence.

"How are you, Steve?"

He rolled his eyes.

"Well, this is George's senior year, so as you can imagine, we are *very* busy with college applications."

"Does George have any idea where he would like to go?"

"Stanford," he replied casually, sounding bored with the question.

"Wow!" I enthused fawningly. "Good for him!"

Steve went on to tell me that George had already been accepted to the University of California in Berkeley. He explained that since George had tested in higher than the one percentile, he was begged to apply his junior year.

"That sure takes the pressure off!"

Steve shook his head dismissively. "Well, it would if he wanted to go to Cal!"

I forced a feeble laugh and smirked in mock agreement.

Mercifully, the teacher started his talk. As we left class, I wished Steve well and told him to say hi to George. He did not ask about Matthew, who was probably long forgotten by him.

As we drove home, I shared my Steve story with Peter. What an ass. Sure, we were also guilty of letting Andy's talents give us a boost, but at least we didn't brag about him. Did we?

Once home, still wounded, I looked for Andy so I could tell him how proud I was. I found him in his room, talking to Matthew on the phone.

"You *did*? That's great, Matthew," Andy was saying. "I sure can't build a motor. Will you teach me when you come home for

Thanksgiving? And guess what?"

I backed out of Andy's room. I could talk to him later. He was busy talking to his big brother.

CHAPTER 38

THE VISIT

IT IS NOT A PERFECT WORLD. It was June, and the end of Matthew's second year at Camphill. As one of the higher-functioning students in the class, he was the lead in the year-end play, *Faust*, and family from California to Connecticut congregated in the school's theater to see his performance. Following the play, Matthew was scheduled to come home for two weeks, and then return to Camphill for a monthlong summer camp. After camp, he would come home again for five weeks before returning to Camphill for his third year.

We thought it was ambitious for Matthew's teacher, Guy, to tackle a play that, even when modified for the Camphill crowd, is very challenging. But Matthew was an impressive Dr. Faust, and we were amazed at his command of his, and everyone else's, lines.

Tyrone, Matthew's friend with Down syndrome, is nonverbal. Wearing a red cape that he swished around like a matador, he played the Devil, gesturing his lines while a teacher's aide hid behind the curtain and spoke them. Matthew's love interest in the play, Emma, a beautiful blond with cerebral palsy, had periods when her ability to speak ceased, and she rocked onstage, struggling to find her voice. Matthew waited patiently while Guy crouched in front of the stage, clapping his hands rhythmically while whispering her lines, a trick he had devised to get her back on track.

At one point in the play, one of the students in a bar room scene simply walked offstage. Guy, participating in this particular scene, jumped up, slapped him on the back and ad-libbed, "Got to get back to the wife, do you, mate?"

John once said that Matthew would be good-looking if he weren't autistic. As unkind as that sounds, I knew what he meant. At seventeen, Matthew had grown into a handsome young man, with a tall, wiry frame, broad shoulders, and sandy blond hair. His expressive eyebrows frame his brown eyes, and his jaw is square and masculine.

But his exaggerated expressions and body carriage give him away. His forehead twists with intensity and he smiles too suddenly, too widely. There are moments when he appears to have it all together, but then breaks into a hand-flapping, jumping-and-dipping flurry of activity, a reaction to being overstimulated by his environment and his mysterious internal world.

On the night of the play, however, Matthew was poised and fluid in his movements and had a composure we rarely see. It was an emotional evening, triggering tears of pride throughout the room.

With *Faust* behind us, we looked ahead anxiously to the next couple of weeks when Matthew would be home.

We always braced ourselves for these visits because even at

their best, transitions made Matthew frantic. Prior to a visit home, he made elaborate and detailed mental plans, such as hanging out with his friends. The friends he had in mind were the kids who once made fun of him, and their attention, though negative, was sadly mistaken for friendship.

There was Jack, the football player, who acted like Matthew's pal when I was looking, only to turn around and taunt him into pulling his pants down in public or encouraging him to ask out a girl he knew would rebuff Matthew. And he dreamed of spending time with the girl he had a crush on, who had gone to the principal in both middle school and high school, complaining that Matthew was stalking her. And indeed he was, peeking at her through windows as she tried to concentrate on her classes, chasing her down at breaks and at lunch, begging for attention and calling her incessantly.

"Matthew, leave her alone! She thinks you are nice, but you are bothering her. Give her some space!" we'd say.

"But I like her!" he replied in anguish. You can't tell a desperate person with no social understanding to play hard to get.

When plans did not go as he had anticipated, things got complicated.

We worried particularly about the fact that Andy, now sixteen, had his driver's license. Some autistic people learn to drive and get a driver's license, but it was clear to us that Matthew would not be one of them. This bothered him—a lot. Desperate as always to be a regular guy, he was infuriated that his brother, who was *two years younger*, could drive and he couldn't. To make matters worse, it seemed that every person he'd known since preschool was driving, even some of the special-ed kids. He argued with us that he had been reading the Pennsylvania driver's manual and therefore he could drive. He even made himself a driver's license from a Ford dealership card he'd found. He wrote his name in indelible ink on the license plate of my car to prove his eligibility.

We had learned that the best way to deal with Matthew was head-on. "You can't drive because you are autistic," we would say. "You are a great kid, but it would not be safe for you to drive a car."

He already knew this, of course. But looking at his tortured face and hopeful eyes was heartbreaking. After one of our many discussions on the subject, Matthew pleaded with us to fix his brain so that he would not be autistic. My motherly response was that I loved him the way he was and wouldn't want to change him for the world. I went on to tell him of all his talents that his two "normal" brothers did not possess—Andy is not a good gardener, John can't cook pancakes the way he can. His tearful response was that being autistic meant he couldn't drive.

A few days after Matthew came home, things were going especially well. Andy was in his room, talking to his girlfriend on the phone, and John was playing with a friend in the backyard. Matthew was in a really upbeat mood. He had just mowed the lawn and asked if he could wash my car. I thought this was fine and perhaps a good chore to distract him from his lawn-care fixation. He thoroughly washed the car, which we had locked, keys hidden. We praised him enthusiastically, and he rewarded us with one of his wide, honest smiles.

He asked that since he had done such a great job, could he

please drive the car five feet into the garage. His only experience with driving up till then had been in the parking lot of our local church in Peter's car, with Peter's hand planted firmly on the emergency brake. We knew that this concession could further inspire Matthew to pursue his driver's-license mission, but we were worn down by his petitioning.

In a moment of weakness, I asked Peter to sit in the passenger's seat of my car while Matthew moved the car into the garage. I stood in the driveway and, already wondering what we were doing, watched Matthew get in the driver's seat. As he started the car, Peter, who was not familiar with my car, asked, "Where is the emergency brake?"

In slow-motion horror, I watched the car plow into the garage wall, crushing a number of full paint cans in its path and destroying two bicycles. Paint was everywhere. No one was hurt.

Andy, whose room shared a wall with the garage, ran out of the house looking dazed. "There is a big hole in my wall."

As we cleaned up, surveying the damage in stunned silence, Matthew said that maybe he shouldn't drive till he was twenty-one. John offered to pay for the damage with his allowance money. And Andy resumed his conversation with his girlfriend. I told myself that this incident was actually a good thing, as surely it would keep Matthew from driving again and possibly getting hurt.

I shared this wisdom with Peter who had been mumbling, "I can't believe what idiots we are." We both recognized our lapse in judgment. We also knew that we had been driven to this lapse by our desire to keep the peace and to try to help Matthew feel like a regular eighteen-year-old.

Matthew's remorse following the incident was genuine. We believed he would share our logic that this mishap proved that he should not drive the car this summer—or ever. We hid all extra car keys and kept the ones we needed with us, either in a pocket, a sock, or a bra.

In the days that followed, I kept Matthew very busy. He mowed and edged our lawn compulsively, and a few of my nice friends invited him to do the same at their homes.

One of those days, I got a frantic call from my friend Dorothy. "Something has happened," she said.

I braced myself, ready for action. It turned out that Matthew had been weed-whacking near her car, causing a rock to fly through the rear window of her van, shattering it. I drove over, calmed everyone down, called a mobile unit to come replace the window, and brought Matthew home. I must have set my keys down for a second.

"Matthew?" No answer. The house was deadly quiet. "*MATTHEW?*" I yelled out the back door. I walked out my front door and noticed the garage door was open. The car was gone. I ran down the street shouting Matthew's name. We live around the corner from a middle school, and I thought he might have driven there to show off. Sure enough, there was my car parked cockeyed in the parking lot, Matthew standing nearby looking scared, hugging himself, his hands grabbing his shoulders, his head down. I was familiar with this stance.

It was as if he were trying to hold himself together.

Somehow, I got Matthew back in the car and drove him home. I knew it was important that I choose my words carefully when scolding Matthew. Keep it simple, I thought. Don't lose control.

Matthew sat across from me in our living room with a nervous smile, tears pouring from his eyes, waiting. I was still out of breath from running, and from the horror of what could have transpired.

Finally, I said, "I am very angry with you right now."

"Well, I'm angry with you for yelling at me in front of all those hot girls!" he shot back.

Toward the end of the second week of Matthew's visit, we were all looking forward to his departure. At this point, it had become a matter of safety that he return to Pennsylvania and to the capable hands of Camphill, where he fit in. It was frustrating to us that Matthew did so well there only to come home and create such turmoil. It would be so nice if *we* could enjoy the fruits of his growth at school.

I became preoccupied with finding a better way to ease this transition in the future. I could hire "friends" for Matthew to hang out with—a couple of guys, a couple of girls. Later in the summer I tried this until Matthew became obsessed with a few of the kids, calling them several times a day, driving them away. I overheard a telephone conversation in which Matthew was explaining to the mother of one of the girls that he was *so* lonely. The mother replied, "Why don't you call some of your friends?"

At the end of the two weeks home, it was my turn to fly Matthew back to Philadelphia. Matthew always sat a few rows ahead of me when we flew, in a window seat. This was set up in advance. In the special-education community, we call this shadowing—supervising as invisibly as possible and being ready to intervene if anything went awry. Once the plane took off, things almost always went well. On these trips I was anxious about who his seatmate would be, and how I could explain the situation without upsetting them.

Matthew liked to travel with his ninth-grade yearbook—from the only year in which he had attended regular high school. He used it as an icebreaker. When he saw someone he wanted to talk to, he'd open his yearbook and show his seatmate pictures of his "friends." Ironically, even as he attempted to prove that he was a regular kid, his social awkwardness advertised his disability.

Matthew did not like to travel with me. He refused to stand near me and didn't want me to look at him. He wanted to appear like a regular guy traveling alone. This was a big problem when we got to security.

"Here, Matthew! Show the lady your ID!" I said cheerfully.

"*Don't look at me!*" he yelled, clutching his yearbook.

It didn't help that he was wearing brown socks with sandals and a SpongeBob shirt, and that his fly was down.

"Pull up your zipper," I whispered.

"Go away!"

Everyone was looking nervous. I quietly told the screener that Matthew was autistic, which I think she had already figured out.

"DON'T TALK ABOUT ME!" he shouted.

Somehow we made it through, and I offered Matthew an Ativan, a mild tranquilizer my pediatrician had recommended for tense times like this. He took it with no argument. When we got to the gate and began boarding the plane, Matthew glared at me and said, "I am not someone to be messed with!" I guessed the Ativan hadn't kicked in yet.

Trying to make light of this comment to comfort my fellow passengers, who looked increasingly ill at ease, I replied with a chuckle and a friendly hug, "Oh, don't I know it!"

"*Don't touch me!*" was his reply.

We found our seats, and I tried to get a look at Matthew's seatmate. I was extremely tense and avoided eye contact with my fellow passengers, whose anxious eyes were all on me, or so I felt. I gave the flight attendant my speech.

"The young man in 18F is my son and he is autistic. He will be fine once he settles down. Please let the passenger next to him know, and I'm happy to answer any questions."

I tried to sound reassuring, but I was too keyed up to reassure anyone. The flight attendant smiled at me compassionately, and I could feel my eyes filling up.

Right before takeoff, a round woman in her forties approached me. She had a short frumpy haircut and glasses. Her face was pleasant, but she looked nervous. She was Matthew's seatmate. She said she had heard about autistic people, but what should she do? What should she say? Is he brilliant like that guy in *Rain Man?*

I told her that he probably wouldn't talk much and would look out the window most of the time. I asked her to let me know if there was a problem.

Things did settle down once we were in the air. I spied on Matthew from time to time but could see only the top of his head. The flight attendant stopped by a few times and told me he was doing great. I casually glanced in his direction on the way to the bathroom, and his seatmate gave me thumbs up. I even dozed for a while, and everything seemed under control.

Matthew and I found each other after filing off the plane in Philadelphia. The plan was to meet Christophe, the German student who worked at Camphill; he would take Matthew to the school and I would turn around and fly home. I usually rented a car and delivered Matthew to school myself and spent the night, but I was needed at home by the rest of my family, who were still all reeling from the agitation of the last couple of weeks.

As we looked for Christophe, I heard running footsteps and a breathless voice calling "Matthew's mom! Matthew's mom!"

I turned around to find Matthew's seatmate with a big smile, looking exhilarated.

"Matthew was great!" she exclaimed. "He talked to me the whole time and showed me his yearbook. He wanted to know all the states I had been to. He is so nice! It wasn't at *all* what I expected!"

Matthew loped excitedly toward baggage claim, looking for Christophe. When he saw him, his face lit up with a smile. Once it was time to say goodbye, Matthew let me hug him, and then he pulled back and looked at me, still clutching his yearbook.

"Don't cry, Mom. I won't be gone that long." Off he went with Christophe. I watched the two walk away until they disappeared down the escalator toward baggage claim.

CHAPTER 39

SPRING BREAK

MATTHEW'S SECOND WINTER in Pennsylvania was long.

"I'm a gardener!" he wailed to me on the phone every week between October and March. "I can't do my work if it's raining and snowing all the time!"

"It'll be spring break before you know it," I reassured him. "We'll have a lot of work for you to do then."

———

It is day five of Matthew's spring-break visit. Here is how the day unfolds.

I am lying in bed at 6:30 a.m., waiting for Matthew to stir. Peter has left for work, and John and Andy are off skiing with friends.

At 6:31, I hear the front door slam. Matthew has gone out to watch some gardeners working a few houses down. It is a cold, drizzly morning, but I know he's wearing shorts and a T-shirt that reads SHUMAKER LANDSCAPING with our phone number below.

At 7:30, I'm up and ready for Matthew's breakfast ritual. He will make pancakes, stack them on a serving plate, then go into his room to sing a song and say a morning prayer.

Just like at Camphill.

After breakfast, Matthew tells me his plans for the day.

"First, I am going to the mall with Ben, then I'm going to work at Dorothy's."

My friend Dorothy had always assured me that she was available to help with Matthew.

"Matthew, Ben is on spring vacation, and I don't know about Dorothy. I'll call her. But first we have to go to the dentist."

Matthew insists on calling Dorothy. He knows that he is more persuasive than I. After a few minutes, he hands the phone to me.

"Sure, Matthew can come work in the garden. But first I'm waiting for the vet to come to euthanize the dog." I tell her how sorry I am. Perhaps Matthew can work for her another day, but Dorothy says today would be fine, *after* they have taken the dog away. We decide not to tell Matthew about the dog or he'll ask questions—"How old was Copper? Where was I when he died? What was I doing? What were you doing when the dog died?"— oblivious to distraught family members' feelings.

I drive Matthew to the dentist, and he tells me to wait in the car; he wants to go in himself like a regular man. After thirty minutes, he comes out. The dentist would like to speak to me. Matthew follows me in and sits in the packed waiting room while I talk to the dentist. It turns out I need to schedule a time to have Matthew's wisdom teeth removed.

On my way out, I see that Matthew is intently reading *The Care Bears Go to the Dentist*. By the expression on his face, you'd think he was reading *Paradise Lost.*

"Time to go, Matt."

"I'm not finished with my book. I'll meet you in the car when I'm finished."

I scan the faces in the waiting room, all stifling laughter. I flash an embarrassed smile and walk out to my car.

After five minutes, Matthew gets in the car.

"Can we call Dorothy now?"

"No. She said she'd call after her . . . doctor's appointment."

It's 9:30. The dog is to be put to sleep at 12:30. I need to keep Matthew busy for three and a half hours so he won't pester the grieving family.

He goes to work in our backyard, mowing, trimming, blowing, and raking while I do laundry, pay bills, and vacuum, stopping every ten minutes to check on him. At around 11:30 Matthew stomps into the house, his shoes caked with grass clippings.

"We need to go to the hardware store. I need oil for the lawn mower."

Off we go. I walk in with him but give him space. As he appears with the oil, I realize I don't have cash and will have to pay with a credit card.

I approach Matthew, and he yells, "I'm a regular guy! Let me buy this myself!"

"You're a regular guy with no money, and you need me to pay for this. Be quiet."

He points at an elderly man in line. "You don't see *him* shopping with his mother!" Matthew shouts, and once again, I'm onstage.

"Shape up," I say, "or we'll leave the store and there will be no more gardening today."

We pay, and as we walk out, the motherless elderly man winks at me sympathetically, a slight kindness that makes all the difference in my day.

At home, I take a moment to fold some laundry. Matthew enters the room, looking shifty. "Dorothy called," he lies.

"Did *you* actually call Dorothy?"

"How did you know?" he counters, looking sheepish.

"I just know," I say with a sigh.

"She said we can go over now."

I call Dorothy to verify the facts. The lifeless dog is being carried away on a stretcher at the moment. Could we wait a little while?

I hold Matthew off till 2:30, about an hour postmortem. Dorothy's twelve-year-old boy is mourning in his room, and her teenage son and daughter bravely greet Matthew, who tells them, "You better *big-time* not mess with me."

Dorothy tells me I look tired, and we talk briefly about Copper's final hours. I promise to pick Matthew up at 3:45, then I drive home and collapse on the couch, waking at 3:30. Time to get Matthew.

"Did it go all right?" I ask Dorothy, and she shrugs. Matthew gets in the car and announces that he is in a bad mood, and that we are not going to talk about it.

Once home, Matthew goes in his room and listens to music— his favorite, the Beatles. I plop down on the couch and turn on *Oprah*. Lisa Marie Presley and her mother are guests. The mother has had a lot of work done, and she looks younger than her daughter in a freakish way. What's with her upper lip? I hear Matthew emerging from his room, and he comes in to see me, tears rolling down his face.

"Do you hear this song?" he asks. I listen, and I hear Paul McCartney singing mournfully, "All the lonely people / Where *do* they all belong?"

"Am I kind of like Eleanor Rigby?" he chokes.

"Awwww," I reply, rocking Matthew in a hug, telling him it hurts to be lonely, doesn't it, and reassuring him that he belongs, is needed, is loved. I feel a pain in my chest, the kind of pain a mother feels when she knows she can't fix an aching heart.

"Who loves me?" he asks, sobbing.

I tell him a long list of all the people who love him. I tell him to go wash his face, and while he does, I call Peter, my father, and my brother, and ask them to call Matthew and tell him how great he is. They do, and Matthew recovers. He makes plans with all three men—going out for pizza with Dad, going to the beach with Grandpa, working with Scott in his garden. I am so grateful for all of them, and proud of Matthew for pulling himself together. Soon, he is in the backyard, removing a patch of lawn, raking and sweeping. I take a deep breath. Now what?

Peter comes home at 6:30. Matthew shows him all the work he has done today, so proud. The two of them joke around about poisonous plants. After a while Peter comes in and comments that our lawn is clipped like a putting green. He tells me I look tired and gives me a hug, and we sit down to a scrounged-up dinner: dry chicken breast, toast, and carrot sticks, washed down with good wine. I go over the events of the day. By the time I get to Priscilla Presley, we are in hysterics. Matthew appears before us and tells us to stop laughing.

Matthew dines on warmed-up spaghetti and spinach salad. He bathes and settles down for the night. I sit on the couch and watch *American Idol* in a daze while Peter and Matthew listen to the Beatles, their evening ritual, before Matthew goes to sleep.

The phone rings, and it's for Matthew. It's Ben, and he's back from spring break. Does Matt want to hang out tomorrow? Maybe go to the mall or something? I sigh, my heart full of gratitude, and Ben tells me, "Don't even *try* to pay me."

Peter and I catch the end of *American Idol*, and I tell him I'm sorry I'm not more talkative, I'm just so tired. He understands. We go to bed and read. After three minutes, my book drops to the floor, and I drift off. Not such a bad day. Maybe Matt will sleep in tomorrow.

CHAPTER 40

COURT PROCEEDINGS

WHENEVER MATTHEW WAS HOME from Camphill, there was business to take care of. During Christmas break, we scheduled his annual physical. At Thanksgiving, he got a haircut and visited the dermatologist. During spring break, it was time for a visit to the dentist.

But this last spring break, as Matthew was turning nineteen, we had some very important business to take care of. A court investigator was coming to visit our home. Peter and I were in the process of obtaining limited conservatorship for Matthew, as advised by the Regional Center caseworker who had been involved with our family since Matthew's autism diagnosis years ago.

Limited conservatorship would enable us to continue to care for Matthew as we had since birth, making decisions about where he would live and about his education. We would continue to be in charge of his financial affairs and medical treatment. We could give or withhold consent should he decide to marry.

We had endured many painful steps since Matthew's birth—diagnosis, search for treatment, and yearly evaluations by the school and state, to name a few. But this step was particularly difficult. It was an admission that after all of our years trying to build skills and autonomy, our adult son would not achieve the independence of which we, and he, had dreamed.

The attorney assigned by the court to represent Matthew had come to call the day before. Both the court investigator and the attorney were required to make home visits to verify that Matthew was indeed disabled enough to warrant this drastic action, and to advise him of his rights. The attorney, who later would admit that Matthew's was only her second such case, was a young blond without a line on her face. With her businesslike, slightly suspicious manner, I felt like a scam artist looking to bilk my son out of his rights and freedom.

We chatted briefly at the dining room table, my attempts to break the ice ("I love your briefcase!") falling flat. Then she asked if she could meet Matthew alone. I coaxed him from his room, where he was studying a book on poisonous plants, and I eaves-dropped on their conversation from the kitchen.

"Do you know that I'm an attorney?"

"What's that?"

"Do you have a driver's license?"

Ooooh, sore subject. Wants one. Can't have one.

"Do you have a girlfriend?" Silence.

You're on a roll. Why don't you ask him if he has any friends—at all?

"Do you know how much a car costs?"

"A lot of dollars."

"Do you know how much a hamburger at McDonald's costs?"

"No."

He doesn't go to McDonald's.

After asking him a few more questions, she told me with a wink that we clearly had a good case. She didn't know that I was on the verge of crying, and that I was desperate for some kind of reassurance that I was doing the right thing.

I knew that the young attorney meant no harm, but she had frayed some nerves and uncovered some insecurities. I worried that another grilling might damage Matthew's ego, and mine.

A few days later, while waiting for the court investigator to arrive, I paced anxiously, wringing my hands. I envisioned a stout jail-warden type with frizzy dark hair pulled back in a tight bun, and I worried that she would bark at me and I would dissolve into tears. So when I opened the door to Claire, the court investigator, I was utterly relieved.

Claire had a shy, sympathetic smile, an open face, and brown Labrador-retriever eyes. Her brown hair was spiked in a youthful boy's haircut and she wore a bright orange Oxford shirt and khakis. The only thing that distinguished her from a younger sister happy to see me was the badge that she wore around her neck.

I showed her to the dining room table where the attorney had needled Matthew a few days earlier, and she immediately reassured me that her visit was routine and that our case was straightforward. She explained the process and encouraged me to ask questions. Claire treated me like a heroic parent going to great lengths to secure the uncertain future of my challenged son. At that moment, Matthew emerged from his room with a long piece of toilet paper streaming from his left nostril. Why hadn't he treated the attorney to such a greeting? He might have been spared the driver's license and girlfriend questions. Claire asked Matthew if she could see his room, and as before, I listened from the kitchen while she explained her visit.

Matthew took it all in somberly, and then told her he could take care of himself. "I'm good at hard things," he said proudly.

"I can see that! Wow!"

I peeked in and saw him proudly holding up the checkerboard that he made in woodshop.

"Let me look at this!" Claire turned it over in amazement and felt its well-sanded corners. Matthew studied her face while she admired his work; his smile and chuckle were infectious and heartbreaking. I could tell Claire felt it, as her voice cracked while she explained that being taken care of by your parents is a good thing.

"Your mom seems really nice. I'll bet your mom and dad are so proud of you." Then she asked him if he had any questions.

"What states have you been to?" he asked his new friend. Claire patiently recounted all the states she could remember, and listened in amazement to Matthew's list.

Sobbing like an idiot from my spying post in the hallway, I quickly dried the tears with my sleeve when Matthew emerged from his room with Claire and walked her to her car.

"Back off!" he told me as I followed them out. Claire smiled and nodded—we were done. Another dreaded visit. Another bittersweet ending.

Claire's name is on the top of my Christmas card list. I wonder when her birthday is?

CHAPTER 41

ALONE

THE MORNING OF MAY 22, 2006, I set my alarm for 4 a.m. I wanted to be the first one to wish Matthew a happy birthday. He answered the house telephone on the first ring. He knew I would call.

"Matthew!" I said. "You're 20! Can you believe it?"

"Yes," he responded flatly. "But Mom? I have something very important to ask you. I've been thinking about Amy. Can we go see her?"

Matthew had met Amy three years before during his first year at Camphill. Like Matthew, Amy is autistic. The staff at the school had told us that they liked each other a lot and we were thrilled; since Matthew's diagnosis years ago, we grieved at the thought of him living a solitary life.

By the time Matthew became interested in girls, he picked the "normal" ones—those who showed him even the slightest kindness, smiling at him in the hall at school or helping him as tutors in his special-education class—and he trailed them relentlessly. He would cry and sometimes yell at them if they told him to back off, and no amount of coaching helped. We were thrilled that the school community nurtured and supervised his friendship with Amy.

Amy's parents were also excited about the budding relationship, and since they lived near the school, they were able to observe and support the autistic lovebirds.

"They are beautiful together," said Katie, Amy's mother. "They go for walks and talk, sometimes sitting on the garden bench. Amy doesn't like to be touched and Matthew respects that."

Contrary to popular belief, not all autistic people are averse to touch, and we were surprised that Matthew, who had been known to approach women of all ages and ask them if he could put his arm around them, or touch their hair, could restrain himself. I had shared this information with Katie and the school staff.

"So keep your eye on him!" I laughed nervously.

"Oh believe me, we do!" they reassured me.

Amy's parents sent a picture of the young pair together, and they were a striking couple: Matthew, tall and blond and wiry, with broad shoulders and brown eyes, and elfin Amy, short and slight, with long brown hair and pale blue eyes. The pair stand side by side, looking down and smiling slightly. "Amy doesn't usually let anyone stand that close to her," said Katie.

A few incidents in the course of the relationship kept us on edge, as when Amy refused to see Matthew for a week after he pushed her into a swimming pool fully clothed, and the time he followed her into the bathroom and locked the door.

"Did he do anything?" I asked the staff, my heart racing.

"No, he just watched her going to the bathroom."

Whatever we are paying these people, it's not enough.

While news of these missteps was unsettling, we felt fortunate that the staff remained calm. They used the episodes to teach Amy and Matthew appropriate rules of relationships. Everyone began to believe the relationship could last, and wouldn't that be *great?*

But a few weeks before the end of the school year, Katie and Sam, Amy's father, took the two out to lunch to celebrate Matthew's birthday. Just as Matthew was opening a gift that Amy had picked out especially for him, he asked the group if they knew *Katherine.*

Katherine was a student-teacher-in-training who had been visiting the school for the last few weeks. I had heard that she was very attractive, and that Matthew was taken with her.

"She is probably better-looking than Amy," he said. "I might like her better."

As a person who would rather endure great pain than hurt anyone's feelings, I was mortified when I heard about his comments. But Katie and Sam found them amusing and said that Amy didn't take them personally. I didn't want to ask whether they thought that Matthew was dumping Amy.

"If we could all be more straightforward, the world would be a better place!" they said, but I was more in favor of polite avoidance and gracious reserve. Unfortunately, Matthew will never be subtle. His brain is wired for brutal honesty.

Peter and I flew back a few weeks later to pick up Matthew for the summer break, and we asked him if we could meet Amy.

"I've moved on," he said, "and we're not going to talk about it anymore." Katie and Sam stopped by to meet us in person, for by now we had already forged a strong connection, having commiserated long-distance about the road behind and ahead. We had laughed about our kids' similar eccentricities and wondered how we could help them connect in a meaningful way.

Though Matthew and Amy parted for the summer dispassionately, we hoped that their friendship could be rekindled in the fall. But the following October, when I asked Matthew about Amy, he reminded me that he had moved on.

"Besides," he said, "she got a haircut, and I don't like it."

———————

In the year since Matthew had last seen Amy, who was now attending a Camphill School in New York, he had complained that there were not enough nice girls around, and that he was lonely. He asked me if I thought, perhaps, that Amy might be lonely, too.

I called Katie and told her about Matthew's request, and suggested that perhaps we could arrange a visit over Memorial Day weekend. She agreed right away. Maybe we could have lunch at their home in Connecticut, and then go bowling and for a hike! I felt like such a good mother going the extra mile to help my lonely son.

Matthew and I drove from Philadelphia to Connecticut and spent the night with family before meeting with Amy and her parents.

"What will we do at Amy's?" Matthew asked.

"We thought it would be nice to visit for a while at their

house," I said, "and then go out to lunch. Maybe we can go bowling."

"No bowling," he said. "When we get to Amy's, all of the grown-ups will talk outside, and Amy and I will go in the house and sort things out."

Sort things out?!

"What do you mean, sort things out?" I asked.

"I want to be alone with Amy in her room with the door shut," he responded.

"But what if Amy doesn't want to be alone with you, and what if her parents don't want you to be alone with her?" I asked, all at once feeling like I was headed for a trap.

"I'll tell them that I'm no one to be messed with," he said, "and we aren't going to talk about it anymore."

It became clear to me that while I was making plans that you might see on a made-for-television movie, Matthew was making plans of his own.

After a brief discussion that escalated into a shouting match, I let the subject drop and called Katie with an SOS before we went for our visit the next morning. The two of us laughed uneasily about Matthew's plan, but decided it would be best to go ahead with the visit.

"We'll just have to be firm," said Katie.

But the next morning, when we arrived at Amy's house nestled next to a pond at the end of a lovely green country lane, there was no walking and talking and standing side by side with slight smiles. Amy, looking adorable in white capri jeans, tank top, and high-heeled sandals, was a bowling pin, and Matthew was the ball, with overwhelming momentum. After the initial greeting where we all told each other how great we looked, Katie suggested that we sit down and catch up.

"Listen," Matthew responded, "I'm the boss today, and I say that Amy needs to be all alone with me in her room."

"But I don't want to be alone with him," Amy whispered to her mom. "He's too bossy."

"Matthew," Katie said calmly, "we are so glad you could visit. But Amy would be more comfortable if we all hang out together."

"No way!" yelled Matthew. "I've been thinking about Amy for a long time! I even dream about her when I'm sleeping, and I want to be alone with her!"

God help me.

"What you are saying then, Matthew, is that you don't care about what Amy wants," Katie said, locking eyes with Matthew. "It's only important what *you* want."

"That's right!" said Matthew triumphantly, like a game-show host moving a contestant to the championship round.

Sam, Katie, and I, all experts in managing autistic melt-downs, gave this visit our best shot and tried all of our tricks, but it was no use. When Matthew made plans, he was determined—obsessed—to see them through, and of course we weren't going to let him have his way.

"Let's go out to lunch now!" I said, desperate to move things along. It was only 10:30.

We all piled into the family's minivan, Matthew leaning close to Amy, and Amy leaning away from him, muttering, "He's bothering me. I don't like it."

During lunch, where Matthew ordered pizza and 21 french fries, Sam, Katie, and I tried to reduce the tension with cordial conversation.

"Matthew, tell everyone where you are going this summer," I said cheerfully.

"I'm not in the mood," he replied. "Let's go back to Amy's."

"Matthew," Sam said, trying to change the subject, "guess where Amy is going this summer?"

"I give up," said Matthew, "and I'm tired of all this talking."

Once back at the house, Matthew announced that he would like to stay a little longer, and then come back the next day, but Sam, Katie, and I, who all looked like we had aged ten years in the last few hours, blurted out reasons why it was time to end our visit—*now*. Somehow I managed to get Matthew back into the rental car, and we drove away. Matthew burst into tears, and when we got to the main road, I pulled over and hugged him.

"They wanted me to stay," he said, "but I'm too busy."

"That's right, Matthew," I said, patting his back. "You're a busy guy."

The next morning, I called Katie and thanked her, and said wow, wasn't that exhausting. She said yes it was, and did I know that Matthew had asked Amy if they could lie down in the grass and do sex.

"Oh, Katie," I gasped.

"She said she didn't want to lie down in the grass because she didn't want to get her clothes dirty and I'm not sure if she even understood what Matthew was wanting. She's still pretty naive."

"Oh, Katie," I repeated, "I am so sorry. Thank you for telling me. Thank you for being so honest."

"And we thought it was difficult when they were young," Katie sighed.

I decided to call to David at Camphill, who had helped guide Matthew with his relationship with Amy from the beginning. In addition to being Matthew's housefather and mentor, he had been Matthew's sex education instructor, and he had a way of explaining things simply and frankly. Matthew had great respect for David and turned to him when he was upset, confused, or simply needed to work something out.

"I'll talk with him as soon as he gets back," said David. "I'll call you and tell you how it goes."

"What did you say? What did he say? Did you get through to him? Should I talk to him?"

David told me that he asked Matthew to tell him about his weekend. "How did it go? How is Amy doing?" he had asked.

"Amy looked nice, but the grown-ups wouldn't let us go in Amy's room and shut the door."

"Did Amy want to go in her room with you and shut the door?"

"Not really. So we went outside and the parents kept watching us."

"Did Amy want to be alone with you outside?"

"I'm not sure."

"Did you touch Amy?"

"I wanted to. I wanted her to lie down on the grass so we could do sex."

"Have you ever had sex with anyone else?"

"Probably not."

David told Matthew what he had heard many times before—but none of it had made sense until today.

"Sex is part of a loving relationship. Both people have to agree to have sex, or it is out of the question. If you have sex, the woman can get pregnant and have a baby. Do you understand?"

"Yes."

"Are you ready to be a dad?"

"No way. I decided I'm not going to do sex with a girl after all."

David reassured Matthew that it was normal for a man his age to want sex, but that there were other ways to satisfy those urges.

"Did you tell him how to masturbate?" I asked, blushing through the telephone.

"Believe me, Laura," David said. "He's already an old pro at that."

He told him that in a few years, when Matthew was older and more mature, he might be able to have a relationship.

"The business of sex and relationships is complicated for all of us," said David. "Matthew needs everyone to support him through this. Just keep it simple, be honest."

I thanked David profusely, and he said you're welcome, "but I'd better get going," he joked. "I've got to keep my eye on Romeo!"

CHAPTER 42

ACCEPTANCE

"HI LAURA. JUST GIVING YOU A HEADS-UP. There was a program last night on this cable channel about miracle treatments for autism. Something about a hyperbaric chamber, and there was another treatment—chelation, I think they called it. They also mentioned the diet thing, so you might be getting some calls. I've already gotten a few. Talk to you soon!"

This first phone message, from my brother Scott, was followed by three others, all from well-meaning friends.

I have grown to dread the news reports on autism break-throughs and the phone calls that followed them because of the way they make me feel. Angry. Offended. Insecure. Guilty.

I feel angry because I have tried so many treatments already: speech therapy, psychotherapy, auditory training, behavior modification, psychotropic drugs. Can't people see how hard I've worked?

I'm offended because they can't accept Matthew as he is. Can't they appreciate his honesty, his humor, and the pureness of his soul?

I'm conflicted. Maybe I should be open to some of these new

treatments. Maybe they will improve his life. I followed every lead when he was young; I tried everything. Have I lost my resolve? Become lazy? Are my weariness and skepticism short-changing Matthew?

I feel insecure because perhaps I haven't done enough, and friends and family think that I could have done more. *"If it were my child —"*

I feel guilty. Just plain guilty. Since he's not cured, maybe I just haven't done enough.

But then clarity returns.

The friends and family who call me about new treatments have seen me struggle through the years and have heard my horror stories. They genuinely want to help. Haven't I shared the good stories, the heartwarming stories, too?

Did I tell them how I lay awake the night Matthew was born just to hear the *squeak, squeak, squeak* of the bassinet being rolled from the nursery with my hungry baby boy?

"Can you leave him here with me now?" I had asked, and the nurse had smiled and said yes. Yes, of course.

Had I shared my joy when Matthew and Andy, at age three and one, ran out to greet their dad home from work with gurgly, contagious laughter? Maybe not. After all, it was a common thing in most families, but precious in ours for the sibling joy and sharing it showed, a sharing we feared was fleeting.

Or the day when Matthew was twelve, and I had scolded him for pushing his brother John into a swimming pool fully clothed. For the first time, Matthew showed genuine remorse. He doggedly repeated his apologies until he was satisfied that he was understood and forgiven. An ordinary occurrence in most families, but a rare victory in ours. Maybe I kept this to myself.

And then when Matthew was fifteen, I went to the skateboard store to buy a shirt for Andy. There was Matthew behind the counter, pretending he worked there.

"May I help you?" he inquired. Matthew's helper, Ben, browsed nearby, pretending to be a customer as well. Have I told others how this made me feel—to see my damaged son trying desperately to be the responsible worker?

The most crippling aspect of Matthew's autism is his social awkwardness. If we could put him in an oxygen chamber and smear him with cream that would suck the metals, good and bad, out of his body, would he become suave and understanding, insightful and clever? Would he learn to read faces and gestures and react appropriately? Would he be sympathetic?

Would he still be Matthew?

Matthew is now an adult, and I accepted long ago that he will not be cured of autism. I want others to accept this, too. It is not easy to be Matthew, someone who wants desperately *just* to be a regular guy. But I admire him for trying.

CHAPTER 43

EPILOGUE

"MOM!" SAID MATTHEW, LOOKING INSPIRED. "I know what I want for Christmas. A thousand-dollar bill! A real one."

Matthew is home for the Thanksgiving break. This year he flew in with Andy, who is now 19 and a sophomore at Yale. Matthew's youngest brother, John, is a high-school freshman.

"A thousand-dollar bill? Why?"

"I want to go to Germany for two days after graduation in June, and I hear it costs a thousand five hundred dollars to go there."

Matthew has been talking about going to Europe for some time, and he's been stacking up his earnings from gardening jobs in the drawer by his bed. Combined with Christmas and birthday money, those earnings are up to $516.68.

I didn't want to deflate Matthew by telling him it actually cost a lot more than a thousand dollars to travel to Europe, or that it seemed impossible to pull off such a trip.

But I sure wanted to find a way to make it happen.

Wondering if perhaps he could visit one of the many German co-workers he'd befriended over the years, I called

Matthew's current housefather at Camphill and asked him what he thought of the idea. He suggested the possibility of a month-long exchange with a Camphill Community in Europe.

"We have a good relationship with a community in England. Jon, the co-worker Matthew works with now, can travel with him. The exchange can be part of his transition plan."*

Besides planning for travel to Europe and beyond, Matthew is eager to move back to California to join Camphill Communities near Santa Cruz. There he'll continue his daily living skills, social skills, and vocational training. David and Onat, Matthew's houseparents from his first year in Pennsylvania, moved to the California Community a few years ago. Since their move west, Matthew has been visiting them during school breaks, and he feels comfortable there. We are happy that he will be just an hour and a half from home, and twenty minutes away from his grandpa in Carmel.

I feel optimistic about Matthew's future. He's become more flexible and reasonable in the last year. We constantly praise him for his maturity, and he fishes for compliments if we don't.

---

* The Transition Plan, a federal requirement mandated by the Individuals with Disabilities Act (IDEA), is designed to prepare students in special education to move from school to adult life. It outlines what a disabled young person wants to achieve in the years ahead and what support he or she will need to live as independently as possible. It covers every aspect of life, including education, employment, housing, health, transport, and leisure activities. Transition planning is based on a student's needs and must take into account his or her interests.

"How am I doing? Who loves me? How smart am I?"

His interests have expanded beyond just landscaping, and he's willing to try new things. He wants to sing in a band, learn how to surf, and go fishing ("only in lakes"). He likes to camp with his dad and his brothers, and he enjoys day trips with me around the Bay Area.

Through the years, friends and family have told me that having a brother like Matthew would make Andy and John better people. In fact, I think they *are* kinder and more tolerant than most. They're incredibly patient with Matthew, enduring his behavior and blow-ups with an equanimity beyond their years.

Peter and I are grateful for the way the community has come to embrace Matthew. People have welcomed him home and asked him, "Please, will you be my gardener today?" When he walked into their store and tried to handle a transaction on his own, they waited patiently while he struggled to count his change. They let him crash a block party, and encouraged him to enter their neighborhood talent show, rewarding him with a prize for his attempt at break dancing. During a recent concert in our town square, the band let him join them onstage and sing, even though he didn't know the words.

"Way to go, Matthew!" they said as they wrapped up the performance.

Raising a child like Matthew and balancing his needs with those of the rest of my family has been equal parts harrowing and illuminating. And every day I have a constantly expanding appreciation of what a struggle it is to *be* Matthew.

During my last visit to Camphill in Pennsylvania, I dropped a plate while I was cleaning up after lunch. It shattered, and I scurried around to sweep up the shards of glass.

"I'm sorry!" I said to the disabled young woman who helped me find a broom and a dustpan.

"That's OK," she reassured me earnestly. "Nobody's perfect."

Not even a regular guy.

ACKNOWLEDGMENTS

I'd like to thank my dad, Phil Bowhay, for inspiring me to write, and Dorothy for encouraging me to join the Wednesday Writers group. I'm grateful to the women in the group—especially our leader, Elizabeth Fishel—who cheered me on and taught me how to find the right words. I'm indebted to Mark Trautwein of KQED Public Radio for being the first to publish my stories, and to Alison Biggar of the *San Francisco Chronicle* for being the second. Thanks to the friends who read and helped edit this manuscript: Dorothy Moore, Joanne Levy-Prewitt, Peter Finch, Steve and Linda Goldfarb, the legendary Alan Rinzler, and last but not least, Peter Shumaker. Alice B. Acheson continues to give much help and encouragement in all aspects of writing, and I thank Book Passage Bookstore for helping me find her. I'm grateful to my agent, Jill Marsal, who worked hard to find a home for my project, and to editor Terri Hinte and designer Linda Kalin, who brought it to the finish line.

Thanks most of all to my husband Peter and our sons Matthew, Andy, and John. We've had our challenges as a family, but you've made the triumphs sweeter.

ABOUT THE AUTHOR

LAURA SHUMAKER is a regular contributor to *NPR Perspectives* and a columnist for *The Autism Perspective*. Her essays have appeared in the *San Francisco Chronicle*, the *Contra Costa Times*, the *East Bay Monthly*, and *Hallmark* magazine, as well as the Wednesday Writers anthology *Something That Matters* (Harwood Press, 2007). Laura and her family live in Northern California.